Technology 2014

Scott Tilley

 *Precious Publishing*
www.PreciousPublishing.biz

ISBN: 1507610467
ISBN-13: 978-1507610466

TABLE OF CONTENTS

DEDICATION

This book is dedicated to my parents. Technology makes their lives easier in some ways, but much more complicated in others. It would be nice if hardware manufactures and software engineers would keep the requirements of the "Greatest Generation" in mind when developing the latest gadgets so that they are usable by everyone.

PREFACE

This is a complete collection of my Technology Today columns from 2014. The column appears each week in the business section of the *Florida Today* (Gannett) newspaper. The newspaper primarily serves Brevard County and the Space Coast region of Florida's beautiful east coast.

The emergent theme of 2014 was **hacks, fracks,** and **quacks**, which was reflected in stories related to computer security, energy innovation, and medical technology. Security vulnerabilities in computer systems affecting multiple sectors were exploited by hackers like never before. Home Depot, Target, and Sony are just a few examples of companies that were in the news for all the wrong reasons.

Hydraulic fracturing (fracking) is an innovative approach to energy extraction that relies on sophisticated technology to access hydrocarbons locked in shale formations deep underground. It's no exaggeration to say that fracking has changed the global socio-political landscape dramatically.

Doctors (quacks) are still waiting for the medical technology necessary to deal with global pandemics like the Ebola outbreak that began in West Africa. We've conquered terrible diseases before; we can do it again.

As with previous volumes in this series, the columns included here are the unedited versions I submit to the newspaper. For each column I include my title, a subtitle that I include as a suggestion to the editors of what they might consider for print and online headlines, and the actual headline used. Any errors or omissions in the book are mine alone.

I hope you find this collection interesting. Please feel free to contact me anytime. I can be reached via email at TechnologyToday@srtilley.com. You can follow my column @TechTodayColumn on Twitter. You can also like me on Facebook at http://www.facebook.com/stilley.writer .

Scott Tilley

Melbourne, FL

Calendar for year 2014 (United States)

January
S	M	T	W	T	F	S
			1	2	3	4
5	6	7	8	9	10	11
12	13	14	15	16	17	18
19	20	21	22	23	24	25
26	27	28	29	30	31	

●:1 ◐:7 ○:15 ◑:24 ●:30

February
S	M	T	W	T	F	S
						1
2	3	4	5	6	7	8
9	10	11	12	13	14	15
16	17	18	19	20	21	22
23	24	25	26	27	28	

○:6 ◑:14 ●:22

March
S	M	T	W	T	F	S
						1
2	3	4	5	6	7	8
9	10	11	12	13	14	15
16	17	18	19	20	21	22
23	24	25	26	27	28	29
30	31					

●:1 ◐:8 ○:16 ◑:23 ●:30

April
S	M	T	W	T	F	S
		1	2	3	4	5
6	7	8	9	10	11	12
13	14	15	16	17	18	19
20	21	22	23	24	25	26
27	28	29	30			

◐:7 ○:15 ◑:22 ●:29

May
S	M	T	W	T	F	S
				1	2	3
4	5	6	7	8	9	10
11	12	13	14	15	16	17
18	19	20	21	22	23	24
25	26	27	28	29	30	31

◐:6 ○:14 ◑:21 ●:28

June
S	M	T	W	T	F	S
1	2	3	4	5	6	7
8	9	10	11	12	13	14
15	16	17	18	19	20	21
22	23	24	25	26	27	28
29	30					

◐:5 ○:13 ◑:19 ●:27

July
S	M	T	W	T	F	S
		1	2	3	4	5
6	7	8	9	10	11	12
13	14	15	16	17	18	19
20	21	22	23	24	25	26
27	28	29	30	31		

◐:5 ○:12 ◑:18 ●:26

August
S	M	T	W	T	F	S
					1	2
3	4	5	6	7	8	9
10	11	12	13	14	15	16
17	18	19	20	21	22	23
24	25	26	27	28	29	30
31						

◐:3 ○:10 ◑:17 ●:25

September
S	M	T	W	T	F	S
	1	2	3	4	5	6
7	8	9	10	11	12	13
14	15	16	17	18	19	20
21	22	23	24	25	26	27
28	29	30				

◐:2 ○:8 ◑:15 ●:24

October
S	M	T	W	T	F	S
			1	2	3	4
5	6	7	8	9	10	11
12	13	14	15	16	17	18
19	20	21	22	23	24	25
26	27	28	29	30	31	

◐:1 ○:8 ◑:15 ●:23 ◐:30

November
S	M	T	W	T	F	S
						1
2	3	4	5	6	7	8
9	10	11	12	13	14	15
16	17	18	19	20	21	22
23	24	25	26	27	28	29
30						

○:6 ◑:14 ●:22 ◐:29

December
S	M	T	W	T	F	S
	1	2	3	4	5	6
7	8	9	10	11	12	13
14	15	16	17	18	19	20
21	22	23	24	25	26	27
28	29	30	31			

○:6 ◑:14 ●:21 ◐:28

Jan 1 New Year's Day	May 11 Mothers' Day	Oct 31 Halloween
Jan 20 Martin Luther King Day	May 26 Memorial Day	Nov 11 Veterans Day
Feb 14 Valentine's Day	Jun 15 Fathers' Day	Nov 27 Thanksgiving Day
Feb 17 Presidents' Day	Jul 4 Independence Day	Dec 24 Christmas Eve
Apr 13 Thomas Jefferson's Birthday	Sep 1 Labor Day	Dec 25 Christmas Day
Apr 20 Easter Sunday	Oct 13 Columbus Day	Dec 31 New Year's Eve

OUT OF SYNC

Changing a car radio station shouldn't be this hard

Published as "Roadblocks changing the radio station"

January 3, 2014 (420 words)

The car won; I lost. It wasn't a fair fight though. It was a rental car, I was driving in an unfamiliar city, and after a very long flight I didn't have much patience. But still, it shouldn't have been a fight at all. I just wanted to change the station on the car radio. Apparently this model did not support that particular advanced function.

The car was built by Ford. I don't know who built the radio, but it was "powered" (if that's the proper word) by Microsoft Sync. I know this because a sign below the radio told me. But that's all it told me. Some instructions would probably have been a better use of space.

There was no knob to change the stations, just a weird joystick-like device that kept rotating through various inputs – none of which worked. There were apparent menu items indicated by underlines, but they were not touch sensitive. Who has time to reverse engineer this sort of user interface nightmare while driving down the highway?

I eventually started talking to the radio, hoping it might show me a little sympathy. "Siri, change the station." Nope, not an Apple iPhone. "OK Glass. Change station to NPR." Nope, not Google Glass either. I began to feel like the time-traveling engineer Scotty from the movie "Star Trek IV: The Voyage Home," where he keeps repeating, "Computer? Computer?" to an old Macintosh. When he's shown the keyboard and mouse, he remarks, "How quaint." My remarks weren't as polite.

This hardware/software combination is a classic example of a poorly engineered consumer electronics device. The user interface was needlessly complicated. It didn't operate like any other radio I've ever used. There's a time and place for innovation, but this isn't it. It would be like an automotive engineer deciding to put the steering wheel on the floor, thinking driving with your feet would be a superior experience for the unsuspecting rental car driver. It wouldn't work, so why do they think it would work for the rest of the control systems in the car?

The alarming thing is that Allan Mullaly, the current CEO of Ford, is rumored to be a candidate to become the next CEO of Microsoft, replacing outgoing CEO Steve Ballmer. Perhaps this will be clarified at the giant Consumer Electronics Show in Las Vegas next week, where both Ford and Microsoft have traditionally had a large cooperative presence. Let's just hope that they're not as "out of sync" with consumers as their car radio is.

CES 2014

Highlights from the 2014 Consumer Electronics Show

Published as "Apple-free CES is still a hit"

January 10, 2014 (436 words)

The sprawling Consumer Electronics Show (CES) is wrapping up in Las Vegas this week. Absent again this year was industry heavyweight Apple, arguably the leader in popular consumer gadgets. But there were plenty of other companies showing off new products in the desert.

Television: Last year, Ultra HD TV made a big splash at CES. This year there were more UHD televisions from all the major manufacturers. It's still questionable whether or not the average person needs so-called "4K" resolution in their home, but it's the next big thing in TV display technology.

And I do mean "big". Some of these monster displays were 120" across. The entire TV is about 6 feet high by 9 feet wide. Forget about putting these displays on top of your coffee table; you should be worrying about how you'll get it through the front door.

There were also some interesting bendable TV screens demonstrated at the show. These screens can provide a better viewing experience by wrapping the edges of the screen slightly inwards. Some smartphones are rumored to be using this technology in the coming year too. Bendable screens are just a stepping stone towards the ultimate TV screen: completely foldable screens that can shrink when not in use and expand when turned on.

Personal Computers: There seems to be a growing backlash amongst some of the manufactures towards Microsoft and their lackluster Windows

8.1 operating system. The manufactures have responded with dual-boot systems that also run the Android operating system. This would let consumers run many of the apps they are familiar with from their phones on their computers.

Blended tablet computers were also popular at CES this year. These hybrid devices can work as a tablet for media consumption, but also as a notebook for typical office tasks. Such computers have been around for a few years now, but they have not really taken off in the marketplace.

Infotainment Systems: There was a time when a car came with a radio, and that was it. Those days are long gone. Today's cars come with infotainment systems, which provide a full range of entertainment possibilities. This includes traditional radio, satellite and HD radio, CD and DVD playing capabilities, MP3 and Bluetooth inputs, iPhone integration, GPS maps, and much more.

Infotainment systems do offer a richer experience for people in the car. But they can also be a terrible distraction while driving. Moreover, infotainment systems significantly increase the complexity of the modern car's dashboard. They are one of the reasons the driver's controls now resemble an airline pilot's cockpit.

Too bad we still don't have flying cars though.

THE AGILE MANIFESTO

The four core values of agile software development

Published as "An agile approach makes a lot of sense"

January 17, 2014 (428 words)

In 2001, Kent Beck, Martin Fowler, Dave Thomas, and 14 other leading software practitioners published the "Agile Manifesto," which was a brief statement of some of the central tenets of lightweight software development methods. The manifesto espouses a "learn by doing" approach to education that is particularly appropriate for project-oriented courses.

This semester at Florida Tech we are offering a special graduate course on agile testing. This is a relatively new area that seeks to combine the best of agile development and software testing. One of the course's learning objectives is to understand how a tester can thrive in an agile environment.

Towards this goal, the students must first understand the nature and origins of the four key values as outlined in the agile manifesto. I think it benefits everyone involved in software engineering to know a little more about the genesis of the agile movement, so that one can place it in historical context. The explanations below of these core values are of course informed by my own opinions.

The first value is, "Individuals and interactions over processes and tools." This speaks to the small team-oriented nature of the agile movement. In small teams, individuals matter a lot, and communication among team members is key. I believe this principle becomes somewhat harder to realize with today's globally distributed development. Processes, and the tools that support them, are less important than people.

The second value is, "Working software over comprehensive documentation." This value is a clear reaction to some of the traditional heavyweight software engineering process models advocated by academics and researchers, such as the Capability Maturity Model (CMM). It's also a reaction to standards bodies that require binders full of documentation that programmers often see as irrelevant to their coding jobs.

The third value is, "Customer collaboration over contract negotiation." This value reinforces the sound practice of involving customers early in development. It also reflects the more open source nature of the early agile movement, where collaboration for joint benefit was seen as more important than financial compensation as recorded in rigid contracts.

The fourth value is, "Responding to change over following a plan." This value is related to the start-up nature of the agile philosophy, where "pivoting" (quickly changing direction) is a common and successful business strategy. Slavishly following an outdated plan clearly makes little technical sense; it only supports an outdated style of project management that incorrectly values milestones over deliverables.

The agile movement is still very strong. Everyone involved in software development should know how agility could affect his or her work – particularly testers.

KINDLE E-BOOKS

Back to the future with self-publishing

Published as "Kindle turns self-publishing on its head"

January 24, 2014 (427 words)

At the end of 2013, Amazon.com reported that nearly 25% of the top 100 Kindle e-books are from independent publishers. The phrase "independent publishers" is a euphemism for self-published authors who have chosen to bypass the traditional publishing process and sell their writing directly to readers.

In the past, we called this sort of publishing "vanity press." As the word "vanity" suggests, it was usually seen as unprofessional: only authors who had their work rejected by "real" publishers would resort to publishing their own work. Implicit with self-published books was the assumption that the writing was of low quality, and the expectation that there was only a very small market for the book – typically limited to the author's immediate circle of family and friends.

Technology has changed all that. Amazon.com's Kindle Direct Publishing (KDP) program has given thousands of authors the opportunity to publish their books their way. Programs like KDP are accelerating disintermediation in the publishing world, and this is having a tremendous impact on the marketplace.

Self-publishing is nothing new. Some very famous authors self-published their books, including Mark Twain, T.S. Elliot, and Edgar Allan Poe. What has changed is the way books are created and distributed. In the past, self-published books still had to be printed and distributed to stores, which was very expensive for independent authors. Today, e-books are digital, which means there is almost no cost for distribution. The KDP platform takes care of the entire process, from uploading your book in Word format to converting it to Kindle e-book format to placing the e-book on Amazon.com's website for the world to buy.

In addition to increased control over their work, self-published e-book authors can enjoy significantly more financial success than most authors who go the traditional publishing route. For example, the KDP program gives authors 70% of the proceeds from the sales of their e-books. This is significantly more than the usual 10% royalty fee paid by traditional publishers.

Last year, the book *Fifty Shades of Grey* by E.L. James became the fastest selling book ever, with over 70 million copies sold in the US alone. This book was first self-published as an e-book. The author is reported to have earned over $95 million, making her the highest paid writer in the business, surpassing even J.K. Rowling of "Harry Potter" fame.

This level of success may not be typical, but technology has put it in reach for more authors than ever before. The e-book market is huge and growing; you only need a small slice of the pie to dine well.

PREDICTING LITERARY SUCCESS

Can computer algorithms replace agent expertise?

Published as "Can software predict which books will sell?"

January 31, 2014 (426 words)

One of the many hats I wear is President of the Space Coast Writers' Guild, a local organization devoted to helping writers of all levels improve their craft. Last weekend we ran the 32nd edition of our annual conference in Cocoa Beach. The conference included agent pitch sessions, manuscript critiques, workshops, panels, and keynote presentations.

A recurring topic in writers' groups across the country is how to get your book published. Some authors are only interested in writing for themselves, perhaps a memoir for therapeutic value or as a legacy for their family. But the majority of writers in the Guild want to see their work published and offered for sale (digital or otherwise).

The challenges with becoming financially successful as a writer are many and varied. Certainly one of them is knowing what will sell well. Traditionally the industry has relied on agents to help in this capacity. Agents use their experience with past success to shepherd new manuscripts to receptive publishers, who in turn use their marketing muscle to get the books they think will sell into the public's hands. Many publishers will only work with agents, not with new writers directly, because agents operate as de facto quality control centers for the industry. Authors rely on agents to guide them towards writing styles and genres that will sell well in today's marketplace.

But what if there was another way to predict literary success? What if a computer program could be used to accurately predict the likelihood of a draft manuscript becoming a runaway success? How might this change the publishing industry?

As reported by *Inside Science*, a recent paper by computer science researchers at the State University of New York at Stony Brook claims to do just that. Their study examines the quantitative connection between writing style and successful literature. They tuned their algorithms using freely available books from Project Gutenberg and other sources. They found that there are distinct linguistic patterns that are shared across multiple books. Their results were impressive: they created predictive models of success with up to 84% accuracy.

Imagine if such an analytical engine were available to all writers now. How would it change their creative process if they knew in advance what sort of writing is more likely to be commercially successful? Would it be a positive influence for them, helping guide their writing more towards what readers want? Or would it be a negative influence, curtailing more exploratory forms of writing that had yet to be experienced by the public?

Maybe we should ask an agent.

FACEBOOK AT 10

What will the next decade hold for the king of social networks?

Published as "Microsoft, Facebook pass major milestones"

February 7, 2014 (431 words)

Two important technology stories broke this week: Facebook turned 10 and Microsoft selected a new CEO. Both companies have had an enormous impact on society. For the younger generation, many of whom cannot remember a time before social media, Facebook looms larger.

Microsoft spent most of its first decade pushing MS-DOS. When Microsoft turned 10 in 1985 it released Windows 1.0. Who knows if Bill Gates thought that the Windows operating system would go on to become the dominant platform of personal computing for the next 30 years.

Facebook spent most of its first decade creating the social media platform now used by over a billion people worldwide. It pushed out competitors like MySpace and bought startups like Instagram to fuel its growth. It's now focused on the mobile marketplace, an area that Microsoft has been unable to crack.

Microsoft had the same CEO (Bill Gates) for the first 25 years. Steve Ballmer replaced him in 2000, and 14 years later Satya Nadella became the company's third leader. Time will tell if Mr. Nadella is able to reinvigorate Microsoft and return it to its former glory.

Facebook's CEO Mark Zuckerberg is also one of its co-founders. As Facebook enters its second decade, it will be interesting to see if Mr. Zuckerberg is able to maintain Facebook's preeminence. If one thinks about Microsoft at a similar stage in its existence, Windows 3.1 had not yet been released, the huge popularity of Windows 95 was years away, and the disruptive technology of the Internet had not yet been felt. Ten years from now we may look back at Facebook circa 2014 with similar nostalgia.

In an open letter to Facebook users marking its 10th anniversary, Mr.

Zuckerberg hinted at what's in store for the company in the next 10 years. A few things he wrote really struck a chord with me. The first was that today only one-third of the world's population has access to the Internet – which means there's still room for the Facebook user base to grow. The second was that the role of social networks will change in the next ten years. Instead of just "sharing moments," Facebook may be used more as a guide and a problem-solving tool. Think of crowd sourcing taken to the next level.

Facebook has already struggled with issues Microsoft didn't have to face, such as data privacy. It will be interesting to see how Facebook reacts when its version of the Internet revolution arrives and disrupts its core business model. It nearly washed Microsoft away in 1995 – near the end of their second decade.

VALENTINE'S DAY

Reach out and virtually touch someone

Published as "Technology can keep you closer to loved ones"

February 14, 2014 (425 words)

Keeping relationships alive when you're far apart is tricky at the best of times. Long distances can create a growing sense of separation and individuality that increases the more time you spend away from your loved one. There really is no substitute for spending quality time together, but technology does offer a reasonable proxy: video chat.

I've used Microsoft's Skype for many years. It's a great (and free) tool to hold video conference calls with people anywhere in the world. It runs on most major platforms and there are app versions to use on your smartphone. It even has a nice feature called Skype Out to make a call to a regular telephone number using Skype for pennies a minute – a life saver when you need to call home while traveling abroad.

As good as Skype is, most of my video chatting is now done using Apple's Facetime. It has a slick interface, it integrates well with other applications, and it works seamlessly with your smartphone. Making a Facetime video call is as easy as making a telephone call, and you can switch from telephone to video anytime.

Skype and Facetime can run on the cellular network, but it's preferable to use a Wi-Fi connection. The signal quality is better and it's free of charge. This means you can let a video chat run as long as you like – all evening if that's what's needed to give you and your partner the feeling of being together even if you're in two different cities.

In fact, many people are now using video chats to share everything they're doing in real time. For example, you can share a meal, even the cooking and preparation, by doing it in parallel with your Valentine: you do it where you are and they do it where they are, but you get to see and hear what each other is doing all the time. It's almost like they were sitting there in the kitchen with you.

You can do the same thing with watching a TV show or a movie. Both of you watch it at the same time, and you can talk about what's happening just like you were sitting on the couch together. (Except you don't have to fight over who gets the comfy pillow.)

This Valentine's Day, if you can't be with your sweetie in person, then reach out and virtually touch them via video chat. It's the next best thing to being there. And you don't have to travel through snow and ice to get there either.

DATA INSECURITY

Another day, another security breach

Published as "More needs to be done to protect our personal data"

February 21, 2014 (430 words)

If there were a new book published called "Privacy and Security," it would be one of the thinnest books on the shelf. That's because there's precious little privacy or security when it comes to our data lately.

Hardly a day goes by without a news story concerning a security breach at a major company, a government organization, or another type of institution. Unfortunately, people are becoming inured to websites and databases being hacked and personal data stolen. But it shouldn't be this way; we should demand more accountability.

Many people know what happened at Target during the last holiday season. Hackers were able to steal millions of records related to point of sale purchases by getting a virus into Target's systems. The investigation by federal authorities is still underway. For customers whose credit information was purloined, Target offered free credit monitoring service. Talk about closing the barn door after the horse has escaped. It would have been less costly, and certainly better PR, for Target to have properly secured their systems in the first place.

In the UK, the National Health Service (NHS) recently admitted that their care.data online storage system could be vulnerable to attack, which would expose personal medical records from millions of people. This risk has understandably caused a lack of trust in the system by doctors and patients, which means many people will choose not to tell their doctors their full symptoms and medical history for fear of it being misused by third parties. The entire program, which would involve automated trawling of doctor records across the country, has been delayed until at least next Fall.

This week it was reported that the University of Maryland's computer systems were hacked, and the personal records for more than 300,000 of its faculty, staff, and students had been stolen. UMD President Wallace Loh said that he was "truly sorry" and that "computer and data security was a very high priority of our University." That's a nice sentiment, but it's demonstrably not true. If security were such a high priority, these breaches would not be occurring so frequently. Taking a page from the Target playbook, the University is offering one year of free credit monitoring to anyone affected.

I fear that breaches like these will continue until the public says enough is enough. If organizations are unwilling or unable to put in place the safeguards necessary to protect our online privacy and personal data, another solution must be found. As much as it pains me to say it, the big stick of costly class-action lawsuits might do the trick.

CUTTING THE CORD

I'm ditching cable for free TV

Published as "TV free from cords, boxes? Life is good for this viewer"

February 28, 2014 (428 words)

As much as I absolutely love dealing with cable companies, I'm finally cutting the cord. From now on, my TV viewing will be from streaming online from sources like Netflix, and free over-the-air signals from the major broadcasters. I'm saying "good bye" to cable TV for good.

Why now? Because the local cable company is forcing me to install yet another device to receive their programming. They are going to an "all digital" format in about a month. I hate having more boxes connected to the TV: more power adapters, more remote controls, more mess.

Moreover, I didn't ask for it. I don't want access to most of the new channels they are offering. In fact, I find TV in general to be a vast wasteland of annoying advertising and ridiculous reality shows that I'm not interested in viewing. I'm certainly not interested in paying for them. Dismal content is no better in HD.

One assumes this change is being made so that the cable company can reduce their infrastructure costs; carrying both analog and digital signals is not as efficient as carrying digital only. But the official reason (according to the literature I received from them), reads like ObamaCare for TV: "We doing this because we know it will be better. You have to switch. Trust us."

But, "better" for whom? The answer should be obvious: for them. Not for me.

So I'm declining their offer and switching to a hybrid viewing model of new and old technology. The new technology is watching most programming streaming over the Internet. There's a small charge to subscribe to Apple TV or Netflix, but the selection is great and there's no commercials. This is the method I use for the majority of my viewing these days.

The old technology is using an antenna. When broadcasters switched to digital signals to support HD, it breathed new life into the antenna industry. Years ago most people used rabbit ears; some homes bristled with large and ungainly antennas on their roof. Today you can use a small antenna and receive free programming from all the major networks. Even here in Melbourne I can receive ABC, CBS, NBC, PBS, and so on, all in clear HD format, for no charge.

The antenna I use is from a US company, Winegard. It cost $60, is about the size of a dinner plate, and is as thin as a piece of paper. It can lie flat or be attached to a wall or window. One cable connects it to the TV and voila – life is good.

BITCOINS

Mining for digital gold in the online Wild West

Published as "Bitcoin isn't reliable as form of currency"

March 7, 2014 (410 words)

Bitcoins have been in the news a lot recently. Some countries have banned then. Large bitcoin exchanges have been hacked. Bitcoin ATMs have started to appear in some cities. Should you use bitcoins?

Bitcoins are a form a virtual currency. Bitcoins are not issued by a central bank, but instead are managed by a decentralized global network. Think of them as tokens used on the Internet, where each token can be used to barter for goods and services online.

One bitcoin is currently worth over USD $600. Their worth is tied to the scarcity of bitcoins in the network. Unlike the US Federal Reserve, which can print money to put more currency into circulation, bitcoins must be "mined" to add to the pool. Bitcoin mining involves solving complex mathematical problems, and each time a problem is solved a few bitcoins are awarded - rather like a miner striking gold, but the complexity increases for the next miner.

Because bitcoins operate in an unregulated peer-to-peer exchange, some people have characterized the bitcoin network as a financial Wild West, and they're not too far wrong. There is no guarantee of security with bitcoins, other than the security built into the ledger system used behind the scenes. There is no deposit insurance, as has become painfully apparent to several people when the largest bitcoin exchange, Mt. Gox in Japan, was hacked to the tune of $500 million.

So why do people use bitcoins? There's certainly a feeling of flouting authority for some users. There are no taxes using bitcoins because there is no national revenue service in charge of them. And because of their anonymity bitcoins have been a favorite currency for all kinds of illegal activity, including money laundering and narcotics purchases on underground exchanges like Silk Road. When countries such as Russia ban the use of bitcoins, you know there's something seriously wild going on.

A few coffee shops and other retailers now accept payment in bitcoins. Personally, I don't use bitcoins or any other emerging online currency. There are enough security risks with regular money to keep my adrenaline flowing just fine.

I don't think bitcoins will survive in their current form, but a new virtual currency will undoubtedly take its place. There is just too strong a demand from the underground market for a digital currency outside the bounds of traditional banking infrastructure and financial regulatory bodies. The new Wild West is online and people are staking their claims.

TURNING 50

How technology has changed society since 1964

Published as "Oh, how technology has changed during the past 50 years"

March 14, 2014 (429 words)

I'm turning 50 tomorrow. Some people say 50 is the new 40; I don't. My body definitely screams 50.

In technology years, 50 is absolutely ancient. We're talking the Eocene era. 50 years ago there were no personal computers, we'd not yet been to the moon, modern medicine was in its infancy, people still read books, and the Internet was not yet invented.

In 1964, "Gilligan's Island" made its debut. Think of the amazing things the professor could make using only salvaged boat parts, coconut husks, and seashells. He was MacGyver's prototype. Today we make apps.

In 1964, Roald Dahl's fantastical book "Charlie and the Chocolate Factory" was published. I read it, and its sequel, "Charlie and the Great Glass Elevator," when I was in elementary school. Today there is still talk of building a space elevator: a very long cable anchored to earth and reaching into space, to be used to reach orbit without rockets.

In 1964, the TV show "The Man from U.N.C.L.E." was first broadcast. It featured two James Bond-like agents, the American Napoleon Solo and the Russian Illya Kuryakin, working together for a UN-like agency, fighting the bad guys around the world. Today we have Edward Snowden, an American who leaked secret NSA documents to the world, being given asylum by Russia. It's unclear who are the good guys and who are the bad guys in this privacy and security mess.

In 1964, the Rolling Stones released their first album. The opening track was called "Not Fade Away," a prophetic title considering the Stones are still going strong after all these years. Today, technology has enabled many people of questionable musical talent to become famous. Social media made Psy's "Gangam Style" a massive hit last year, and the explicit imagery on the video "Wrecking Ball" has made Miley Cyrus hugely popular. Time will tell if they are still making noise 50 years from now.

In 1964, IBM introduced its ground breaking System/360 family of computers. It remains one of the most important moments in computing history. Many of today's seemingly new developments, like cloud computing and virtual machines, can trace their origins back to the System/360. The heart of the System/360 continues to beat today in some of IBM's mainframes, which still run many of the essential functions in large corporations.

Some of the well-known people also turning 50 this year include entrepreneur Jeff Bezos (Amazon.com), author Dan Brown ("The Da Vinci Code"), and actor Keanu Reeves ("The Matrix"). I've been influenced by all of them. But tomorrow I'm going to be channeling Johnny Cash.

AGILE TESTING

Organizational, technical, and behavioral changes are needed

Published as "Agile programmers help ensure crucial testing process is successful"

March 21, 2014 (427 words)

There's a saying that in life you can never been too rich or too thin. Programmers can add, "you can never be too agile," to this dictum. Since most companies are adopting agile software development practices, what does this mean for the practice of testing – and how does this affect you, the consumer?

For a tester to thrive in an agile environment, they need to understand how agile development differs from traditional development. Once they have internalized these differences, they can determine where they can best add value to the team and the customer. Of the many significant differences between agile and traditional development that can affect testing, there are three that warrant special attention: the whole team approach, iteration and automation, and embracing change.

The whole team approach is an organizational aspect of agile development that is central to its success. Instead of having silos of responsibility, in an agile project the whole team is responsible for product quality. The three main groups of people, testers, developers, and business representatives, work together to ensure that the customer's requirements are satisfied. The approach is supported through the daily stand-up meetings involving all team members. For a tester, this is a noticeable change from traditional development: in an agile project, they can exert influence throughout the lifecycle.

Iteration and automation is a technical aspect of agile development that profoundly affects how a tester works. In traditional development, the time between project kickoff and product delivery can be months (or longer). In agile development, a working product is always available (even if it's not functionally complete) at the end of an iteration, which typically lasts from one to four weeks. The time pressures that are always present in testing are exacerbated in agile. This means a tester must rely on a sophisticated technical infrastructure to perform automated regression testing.

Embracing change is a behavioral aspect of agile development that all team members must adopt – testers in particular. Few people like change when it is forced upon them; we react better when we feel in charge. Testers can perform better if they realize that the nature of agile development is rapidly changing user requirements, which in turn dictates rapidly changing test scenarios. Rather than becoming frustrated, testers should build change into their plans and react accordingly.

Testing is important to all of us. When products are not tested properly, they fail in the field. Witness GM's current recall fiasco for product defects they knew were present but neglected to address until it was too late. That's not agile. Or smart.

SYMPHONIC ODYSSEY

STEM+M *in total harmony*

Published as "The M in STEM meant music at KSC concert"

March 28, 2014 (419 words)

Last weekend's "Symphonic Odyssey" by the Brevard Symphony Orchestra at the Kennedy Space Center's Space Shuttle Atlantis exhibit was breathtaking. The music was beautiful and the machinery was awesome. The musicians performed directly underneath the actual orbiter, which hung motionless overhead – a visual snapshot capturing a moment in time when the magnificent spacecraft circled the Earth at over 17,000 mph.

Actually standing just a few yards away from Atlantis, seeing the heat-scorched tiles, the cargo bay doors and robotic arms, and the huge engines at the business end of the shuttle was a dream come true for me; I started writing to NASA when I was a young boy in elementary school student many years ago. It really is rocket science, and who cannot be inspired by such a spectacle?

But it was astronaut (and musician) Winston Scott's speech that really moved me. The concert flyer contained this quote from him: "Rockets and music, each, have transported and transformed me. I am so fortunate to have both in my life." He related how, during one trip into space, he witnessed a rare alignment of planets through the shuttle's windows. He then said a similar alignment of circumstances had enabled him to get into space in the first place. He described how his interest in high school band, coupled with the kindly intervention of one of his teachers who clearly saw potential in young Winston, led directly to a graduate engineering degree and then to a career at NASA – which included two trips into orbit on board the space shuttle.

It's long been known that there's a connection between music and mathematics. Many years ago I had a professor who's PhD was in music, not computer science. He said he felt the two activities were so closely intertwined that a career in both seemed obvious to him. Later on I worked with a scholar doing software engineering research whose first career was as a concert pianist. He brought such a refreshing perspective to solving problems that he was in high demand for important projects.

More broadly, the fields of Science, Technology, Engineering, and Mathematics (STEM) have much in common with music. Indeed, the inside of the back cover of the BSO's regular concert programs feature an advertisement from the Florida Institute of Technology (where I work) espousing "STEM + M: Educating the Whole Mind." To me, there is no conflict between so-called left-brain and right-brain activities. Both are facets of human creativity, and both should be equally developed and exercised.

MACBOOK AIR

The near-perfect combination of form and function

Published as "Lots of thought later, new laptop is just right"

April 4, 2014 (422 words)

It only took me five years, but I finally have a new computer. The cobbler's shoes and all that. Cue the old Alka-Seltzer commercial: "Oh, what a relief it is!"

I had a late-model 2008 MacBook Pro with a 8GB of memory and a terabyte hard drive. It was a great machine, but after countless hours of use and way too many miles on the road, the old computer was slowing down. Literally. It was taking over ten minutes to launch Word. Such long delays are usually signs of a disk drive about to fail, which has happened to me before. I had put off the upgrade for as long as I could; it was time to ditch the old coal-fired steam-powered contraption and catch up with the Jones.

Whenever its time to buy a new computer, I closely examine what's changed in the marketplace. For example, Windows 8 notebook computers didn't exist when I last picked a computer in Spring 2009. They have some interesting characteristics, especially if you get a touch screen model, but the whole Windows experience still seems awkward and frustrating to me.

I considered a Google Chromebook, like the model I selected for my father last year. But my computing needs are rather different than his, and a browser-based device didn't really meet all of my requirements. I'll definitely revisit this decision in the future though – particularly as wireless network access improves and cloud storage becomes more commonplace.

My geeky friends always want me to switch to Linux, but that's a non-starter. I left this DIY operating system long ago; been there, done that. And like it or not, the main software I need is not available under Linux.

So, I decided to stick with Apple. I narrowed down my choices to an updated MacBook Pro or a MacBook Air. In the end I selected a sleek new

MacBook Air, powered by a 1.7GHz quad-core Intel Core i7 with 8GB of memory and a 512GB SDD. At $1,750 it's a tad expensive, but it feels lite as a feather, it's totally silent, and it's crazy fast. The solid-state drive replaces the traditional spinning platters with memory chips, which makes a huge difference in the computer's performance.

I've found the battery lasts over 8 hours with regular usage, which is phenomenal. If Apple added a Retina display and a slightly larger screen, the MacBook Air would be the perfect computer for me. Until they do so, I find it to be the near-perfect combination of form and function.

SOFTWARE RECALLS

Patches are recalls, so why not treat them as such?

Published as "Where's the outrage over faulty software?"

April 11, 2014 (424 words)

The news is full of multi-million dollar fines levied on major corporations. GM and Toyota are the current car companies in the government's cross hairs. Each has been forced to recall millions of cars. Toyota agreed to a record $1.2 billion fine due to unexpected acceleration in some of its 2009-2010 models. GM is being fined $7,000 per day for not complying with NTSB requests for documents related to malfunctioning ignition controls.

Bank of America was ordered this week to pay $772 million in fines and restitution for defrauding 1.4 million customers related to deceptive credit card practices. They are only the latest in a string of financial services companies to suffer penalties for consumer malpractice. I expect more to follow.

One sector you never see issuing recalls or being fined is software. It's ironic that automobiles and financial services companies have become whipping boys for consumer discontent and government punishment, but a huge sector of our modern economy – information technology – gets a free ride.

This is due in part to the fact that there is no equivalent of the NTSB or the SEC for software companies. The federal government and state authorities have little sway over this part of the economy. In cases like this, we usually rely on the market to correct itself: consumers vote with their wallets and stop using shoddy products. But in software, this hasn't happened.

This week the "Heartbleed" security flaw was publicized. It's a massive breach in a program called OpenSSL that is at the center of all secure communications on the web. According to Bruce Schneier, a well-known security consultant, Heartbleed is "Catastrophic. On the scale of 1 to 10, this is an 11." It's used by hundreds of thousands of servers by major corporations around the world. Hackers can exploit the flaw to steal usernames, passwords, and other information that was supposed to be encrypted and inaccessible.

Ironically, there is a word for "recall" in software: patch. Software companies send the repair shop to you, rather than having you to go to the repair shop. They issue patches that are delivered online and applied to the faulty programs. Microsoft is famous for its "Patch Tuesday," where it releases a series of fixes for its products. Every month. Imagine if Ford or Wells Fargo had a "Recall Thursday" every month. They'd never stay in business.

So where's the software recall? Where's the government? Where's the consumer backlash?

It's time to channel Howard Beale from the movie "Network" and yell, "I'm not going to take this anymore!"

THE HUMAN COST OF SOFTWARE ENGINEERING

Until software engineering is fun, product quality will suffer

Published as "Software designers face humdrum life at work"

April 18, 2014 (428 words)

I have often lamented the poor quality of software that we use on a daily basis. The recent Heartbleed security flaw in OpenSSL is just the latest in a seemingly endless series of coding errors and project missteps that cause widespread inconvenience to millions of people. Unfortunately, I think these inconveniences will have to escalate to severe damage and/or loss of life before we will do anything about the human cost of errors in software engineering to society.

But there's another aspect to this problem that should be addressed: the human cost of current software engineering practice on the developers. Perhaps one reason that software quality is so low is that developer's morale is so low. Their incentives for doing good work do not align with management's incentives for quickly shipping a product.

It's human nature to shun things we don't like and gravitate towards things we do like. Any process that attempts to change this fundamental principle is bound to fail. As an example, consider the weight loss industry. Everyone knows that the way to lose weight is quite simple: eat less and exercise more. If we know this fact, why do we have entire sections of bookstores devoted to weight loss books and fad diets? Why do we keep inventing new ways of exercising using Machiavellian machines? Why do we yearn for a simple pill to take care of everything?

The answer is equally simple: no one likes to diet and few people like to exercise. If you liked doing these things, you wouldn't need someone else to tell you to do them. Eventually the external pressure is removed and you revert back to your natural state: relaxing with potato chips and a drink in front of the TV.

It's the same in software engineering. Developers don't like following rigid processes, producing reams of documentation they see of little value, and spending many wasteful hours in boring meetings. So given a choice, they don't do these things. Similarly, many agile methodologies demand a level of sacrifice that developers and testers cannot maintain. A few iterations in a Scrum project are doable, but a constant reduction in sprint time is not possible over the long haul. People burn out.

What we need is a new philosophy of how software is created – one that is actually enjoyable for the developers. As part of our research program at Florida Tech we're working on a new methodology called Curling that is actually fun. After all, software is written by people for people, not by machines for machines. Not yet, anyway.

MICHELIN GUIDE

A venerable brand fails to adapt to the reality of social media

Published as "'Michelin Guide' still is useful, but mostly we've moved
past it"

April 25, 2014 (421 words)

When's the last time you picked up your trusty Michelin Guide to read a
restaurant review? Never? Well, me neither actually. But that probably says
more about the nature of our quotidian dining than it does about the value
of the Guide.

The problem for Michelin, the French tire company that owns the
venerable "red book", is that the dining experience is changing faster than
the Guide. For years, the Michelin Guide was incredibly important to chefs
and restaurant owners. The Guide gives high-end food establishments one,
two, or three stars, with three stars representing the epitome of gastronomic
delight. Adding a star to a restaurant's rating can increase business
significantly. It can make the chef a celebrity – at least for those without
their own "Iron Chef" TV show.

The Guide determines its rankings based on its own anonymous team
of inspectors. These are gourmands (what we might now call "foodies")
with refined tastes and generous expense accounts. Price is rarely a concern;
the overriding concern is epicurean enjoyment. Their readers are people
with financial means who have trusted these inspectors for over one
hundred years.

But these days, people rely less on highbrow printed guides and more
on social media and online services that use reviewers more like themselves
to evaluate a product or service. I can't remember the last time I booked a
hotel on Expedia.com or bought an item on Amazon.com without reading
what others had posted. If there are too many negative reviews, I shy away.

Dedicated restaurant apps like Yelp have replaced the Michelin Guide for the vast majority of today's users. When used with automated booking apps, such as OpenTable, it makes finding the food you want, at the time you want it, so much easier. There is a definite advantage to using location-based services when you're hungry, and this is not something the Guide really focuses on. There is still a market for luxury guides, but it is a shrinking one.

The Guide has been losing money for several years now. In some ways its slow decline is emblematic of a aging brand failing to adjust to market realties. But I think the Guide has been particularly hard hit because of it's unwillingness to acknowledge the changes in it's main customers: people who eat, not people who cook. And these days, there's far more of the former than of the latter. Just take a look at any local restaurant almost any day of the week. Have you seen the lines at Chipotle or Cheddars?

METERED INTERNET

As inevitable as airline baggage fees

Published as "Metered Internet use makes some sense"

May 2, 2014 (421 words)

Do you like your cell phone data plan? If you're like most people, you worry you'll incur overage charges each month by using too much data. But few people really know how much data they use to do ordinary tasks, such as retrieve email or play streaming music.

How much data do you use to watch a video on Netflix?

If the major network carriers get their way, you may soon have to start worrying about Internet overage charges too. In my opinion, metered network access is coming just as surely as airline baggage charges will soon extend to carry-ons.

The current Internet access model is that consumers pay for a certain theoretical maximum bandwidth, which is higher for downloads and lower for uploads. There is usually a cap on overall data downloads per billing cycle, but its high enough that most people never come close to reaching it. In effect, we have an "all you can eat" data plan.

In a metered data plan, you pay for what you use. For people who rarely go online, or who only do low-bandwidth activities such as checking email and browsing the web, this model would probably save them money. However, for people who do a lot online, including video chats and streaming movies, the metered model would probably cost them more.

Would that be so bad? We're already familiar with metered utilities. We pay for the water and the electricity we use. I grew up in a city where the water was not metered; you could use as much as you wanted. No wonder we refilled our 18,000-gallon swimming pool with a garden hose several times a year – it didn't cost anything. But of course it does cost something; the price is hidden in the monthly bill.

Companies like Netflix and Amazon.com are striking deals with the network carriers like Comcast and AT&T to ensure their product receives priority service. They don't want customers to complain when watching a streaming video that is jerky and pixelated, so they are willing to offset the cost of their higher bandwidth use. Many analysts see this as a slippery slope to tiered service and away from "net neutrality," where all data is considered the same.

But again, would that be so bad? We're already familiar with paying for better service for almost everything else in life, from upgraded hotel rooms to theater tickets. When you go to a show, do you prefer "festival seating" or assigned seating that you get to pick – for a price?

SOFTWARE CERTIFICATION

Independent examination based on international standards

Published as "Certified testing builds confidence"

May 9, 2014 (425 words)

I spent this past week at StarEast, a giant conference in Orlando focused on practical software testing and hosted by Software Quality Engineering (SQE). The conference attracts well over a thousand professionals from all over the world who are interested in learning more about current trends and recent developments in software testing. Participants also get a chance to hear from industry leaders through in-depth tutorials, timely workshops, and plenary keynotes. For example, Randy Rice delivered Wednesday's keynote on "Principles Before Practices: Transform Your Testing by Understanding Key Concepts," which was a fascinating talk about the importance of truly understanding fundamental principles to be effective testers.

Participants also have the opportunity to become certified software testers. There are various levels of certification, from beginner to expert. For example, to become an ISTQB Certified Tester – Foundation Level (CFTL), registrants take a 3-day intensive class and then sit the CFTL exam. ISTQB (International Software Testing Qualifications Board) is an international organization that leads the certification effort of software testing competency. According to their website, the ISTQB vision is to "continually improve and advance the software testing profession by defining and maintaining a Body of Knowledge which allows testers to be certified based on best practices."

In the computing field, the two main academic organizations are the ACM and the IEEE CS. But they do not provide the same type of certification that ISTQB does – and which the community clearly needs. Becoming certified is a form of objective validation of one's credentials. The ISTQB exams are standardized assessment instruments. Such exams do have their detractors, but for now they are the best we have. They serve a purpose similar to the bar exam for lawyers in providing society with a certain level of confidence in the profession.

I think examinations are part of the triple-E approach to professionalism, the other two being education (and training) and experience. Students who graduate from a university like Florida Tech earn their degrees, and the value of the degree is backed by the reputation of the granting institution. But the world needs far more testers (and software developers in general) than can go through the university system, and it is for these people that organizations like ISTQB provide a valuable service.

Personally I think software certification is a stepping-stone to professional licensing. Doctors, lawyers, and engineers must all be licensed to practice. Some day, software people will be licensed too, either by choice or by enforced public policy. When licensing becomes necessary, we as consumers may finally have redress when software products fail.

POOL TECH

Why you need an engineering degree to turn on the spa

Published as "Is it on? Pools and spas are remarkable in complexity"

May 16, 2014 (422 words)

According to the calendar, it's still Spring. According to the weather here in Florida, it's starting to feel more like Summer. Before the temperature and humidity both climb into the 90s, if you own a pool you should take some time to learn how it works.

When I first tried to figure out how my pool worked, I felt like I was standing in the middle of a chemical plant, surrounded by PVC pipes, humming pumps and motors, and various electric and gas connections that snaked their way around everything. I literally didn't know where the water went in and where it went out. All I knew was how to turn the system on and off.

Actually I didn't really know that either, because there was no single "on/off" switch. Instead there are three control panels with breakers and mechanical rotors, some helpfully labeled with phrases like "Spa Aux Return" and "DON'T TOUCH!". The latter was written in red ink, presumably from the past owner who had a bad experience mixing salt water and live wires.

The previous pool I owned was very simple. It didn't even have an "on/off" switch. You just pulled out the plug to turn it off. Chlorine was added by placing a puck in the filter. Even I could figure out the simple chemistry needed to understand the water testing kit. But the home leisure industry has fixed these problems by creating pool controls that only a petroleum engineer could love.

Let's say I want to relax in the spa at night. The controls are mostly in the dark, so I get to stub my toes while stepping over various nasty lizards and stinging insects trying to find the right nozzles to turn. First I turn on the pool pump, then I turn on the spa pump (making sure the waterfall pump is off), then I turn on the gas heater for the spa, waiting for the telltale "foosh" sound to indicate that the burner is on (or that the heater is about to explode). Then I turn one knob half-way counter-clockwise, another knob fully clockwise, and then engage in a game of yelling through the pool enclosure, with probing questions such as, "Is it on now?"

There are sophisticated control systems you can buy that hide the complexity of the whole setup. You can manage just about every aspect of your pool, spa, and heater with your smartphone. Which is great – until you drop the phone in the spa while making adjustments to the water jets.

PICTURE HANGING

There ought to be an app for that

Published as "It's time science helps more with hanging art"

May 23, 2014 (429 words)

There are zillions of apps available, but for the life of me I could not find one to help me with the tedious and error-prone chore of hanging pictures. There's an entrepreneurial opportunity here, just waiting for the right developer to make a fortune.

How you hang pictures depends on what type of person you are. If you're an easy-going individual who doesn't mind a few extra holes in the wall, and who is not bothered if the pictures look a little crooked, then your job is relatively easy. You use the tried-and-true scientific method of determining where to start hammering, and by "scientific" I mean you hold out your thumb, quickly eyeball the wall, and just start pounding away.

However, if you're someone who freaks out when a picture frame is tilted by even the teeniest amount, then you need a different approach. This means getting out large sheets of paper, a measuring tape, a laser level, a bubble level, and a calculator. This type of person doesn't trust their aging vision and crooked walls. This type of person uses arithmetic and geometry to solve the picture-hanging problem. I should know: I'm this type of person – and it's not pretty.

Imagine you have two pictures to hang. The pictures are not the same size, so you have to decide if you want the tops to align, or if you want the taller picture to be a bit higher, leaving a bit on the bottom so the shorter picture looks symmetrical. The two pictures are not side-by-side but are on adjoining walls, with a grandfather clock in the corner. The two walls are not the same width either. One picture has two fixed hooks; the other has a wire attached to fasteners. For the wire you need to estimate where the hangers should be placed, keeping in mind the elasticity of the wire so that the top of the frame will line up where you want.

When things get this complicated we usually look for automated help. There ought to be an app that can do all these measurements for us. It should calculate the precise location of where the nails and hooks should be placed. Smartphones have gyroscopes so they can function as levels too. The camera could take photos of the back of the picture and overlay the hooks and wires with mounting instructions, including estimated weight.

All of this is doable; it just a smaller matter of programming. So let the coding begin! And remember, I get 20% of the profit. Call it an idea fee.

SUMMER READING

Book suggestions for budding scientists and career professionals

Published as "As summer opens, so should these books"

May 30, 2014 (414 words)

School is almost out, which means it's time for my annual summer reading list. This year I've selected two technical books, one book on communication skills, and a science-inspired book of fiction that's just fun to read.

The first technical book is for computer scientists and software engineers with an interest in software testing and agile development. The book is called *Agile Testing: A Practical Guide for Testers and Agile Teams* by Lisa Crispin and Janet Gregory (Addison-Wesley Professional, 2009). This is perhaps the best-known book on the subject of agile testing and remains a must-read for anyone working in the area. The agile movement shows no signs of slowing down, so reading this book will help prepare you for the inevitable changes needed for you to successfully manage your software career.

The second technical book is for anyone with an interest in exploring the wild world of neutrinos and particle physics. It's called *The Perfect Wave* by Heinrich Päs (Harvard University Press, 2014). Written in a somewhat autobiographical tone, the book describes various parts of the author's life, including his post-doctoral research and his current work as a professor in Germany. The personal style makes the complex material about heady topics such as relativity, quantum mechanics, and dark energy more approachable. Check out the IceCube project in Antarctica for more information on the elusive and nearly massless neutrino.

The third book is *How to Write Anything: A Complete Guide* by Laura Brown (W. W. Norton & Company, 2014). This book is an invaluable addition to anyone's personal library. Communication skills are absolutely essential to anyone working in a STEM-related field, and knowing how to write various types of documents in a modern style can really help your career. The author provides many examples that you can customize for almost any circumstance, from grant proposals to query letters.

Summer can't be all work and no play, so my final recommendation is a young-adult book suitable for all budding scientists. It's called *The Mad Scientists' Club* by Bertrand Brinley (Purple House Press, 50th Anniversary Edition, 2011). I first read this book when I was in elementary school and it really resonated with me. The stories in the book are a mix of Boy Scout adventures, secret codes and hidden hideouts, and science trickery that the main characters use to their advantage. The author makes science and technology *fun* and for an impressionable youth whiling away the hot summer months, you can't ask for anything more.

ICSE 2014

A glimpse into the future of software engineering from India

Published as "Conference could lead to IT advances"

June 6, 2014 (420 words)

This week the future of software engineering is being discussed on the other side of the world. The 36th edition of the ACM/IEEE International Conference on Software Engineering (ICSE) is being held in Hyderabad, India. ICSE may be an academic event, but the ideas presented there may find their way into the next great startup or your newest favorite app.

When you think of India, you may think of call centers, spicy chicken vindaloo, or maybe the Taj Mahal. India certainly has those things (and much more), but it also has a large and rapidly growing software industry. The city of Bangalore is the largest IT center in India and is sometimes called the "Indian Silicon Valley." Hyderabad is home to more than 8 million people and the Indian base for many of the world's multinational corporations, such as Google and Microsoft.

Traveling to Hyderabad from North America takes more than 24 hours. The weather there this week was a hot and sticky 111F. So is attending ICSE worth it? When I asked a colleague from Carnegie Mellon University in Pittsburgh this question, she answered with an emphatic "yes." She said the country was fascinating, the people she met were friendly, and the topics being presented at the conference were intriguing.

Consider the role of social media and software engineering. How do developers use tools such as Twitter to communicate and share ideas? How do they use websites such as LinkedIn to build a network of professional contacts? This is a hot topic in current software engineering research and the focus of several special sessions at ICSE.

There were several meetings on computing education and the impact of new course delivery vehicles, such as massive open online courses

(MOOC). The inclusion of new technologies such as software-as-a-service and cloud computing in course projects was also discussed. As my own research suggests, there is a constant struggle for instructors to carefully balance the sometimes conflicting goals of academic rigor and industrial relevance in software engineering projects.

ICSE is a venue to present new ideas. One that really caught my eye this year was the gamification of software development. I first heard about this new approach in the context of agile projects. Gamification seeks to make the various activities involved in software engineering fun and competitive, which in turn can improve the overall process by making tasks more transparent. Time will tell if gamification results in better quality software products. Let's all hope so, because there's a lot of room for improvement.

SOCCER WORLD CUP

The beautiful technology behind the world's favorite game

Published as "Advances adding to viewing experience for World Cup fans"

June 13, 2014 (424 words)

Soccer is called the beautiful game in part because it's fun to play and exciting to watch. Most people who follow the World Cup will be rooting for their favorite team and cheering on their favorite players. Being the geek that I am, I'll be pondering the technology behind the broadcast.

The 64 games to be played in this year's World Cup take place in 12 different stadiums spread across the vast expanse of Brazil. Instead of traveling to each stadium, many fans will be viewing the action online. If the recent Winter Olympics in Russia are any guide, the demand for online access to the games will be significantly larger than it was just four years ago in South Africa. This means the technology needed to support millions of online users and thousands of live streams will also be significantly larger.

For the first time ever, the 2014 World Cup is using goal line technology to help determine whether or not the ball enters the net. In the past there have been numerous questionable calls by referees that upon later review were shown to be incorrect. FIFA, the governing body of soccer worldwide, has been reluctant to embrace goal line technology, but with many other sports having successfully adopted it, the pressure was just too much to say no any longer. Let's just hope the technology doesn't fail when it goes live on the big stage.

If you've ever listened to a baseball game on the radio, you know the lulls between the action are filled with player trivia and statistics. For the World Cup this year, broadcasters have access to a treasure trove of "big data" that they can use to provide background stories to the viewers. Powerful computers and software algorithms can analyze all the data available in real time. Since many of the players are not well known outside of their home country, this sort of supplemental information can really help improve the viewing experience – especially since there's only one month in the tournament to learn everything.

If there were one thing I'd ask technology to address for the World Cup, it would be for the broadcasters to use some sort of white noise mechanism to filter out the incredibly annoying sounds of the blaring horns known as vuvuzela. The constant din caused by people in the stands blowing these plastic pipes soon becomes intolerable. In 2010 I had to choose between listening to the commentator or listening to the horns. In the end I think I chose closed captioning.

REAL ESTATE

It's real estate, Jim, but not as we know it!

This column was not published

June 20, 2014 (425 words)

Realtors today are still told that their success depends in large part on the number of listings they have. A listing is a property for sale, with the real estate agent representing the seller. The buyer usually has a different agent, and the two agents split the commission based on the sale price. The more listings you have, the more business is steered your way.

Real estate has traditionally been advertised using the Multiple Listing Service (MLS). The cooperative compensation model for brokers is embodied in it. The public can search the MLS, but much of the valuable information is kept tightly guarded and available only to realtors. This business model worked well for many years, but it's now being disrupted by "big data" technology.

To paraphrase John Lennon, imagine there were no listings. Imagine if most sellers decided not to use a realtor to sell their home, but instead listed it themselves using online companies such as Zillow and Trulia. These "For Sale By Owner" (FSBO) properties already exist, but their numbers could increase substantially if the perceived value of the traditional real estate model using the MLS decreases. Actually it's not hard to imagine, because it's already happening.

It wasn't too long ago that most people used travel agents. Agents controlled access to the airline data: flight schedules, seat availability, and ticket prices. Once companies like Expedia and Travelocity came along, travel agents were disintermediated because consumers could access the data directly. When was the last time you used a real travel agent to book a flight?

Other service industries are also undergoing painful realignment.

Education with open online courses. Taxis with Uber. Publishing with digital media. Once the technology genie is out of the bottle, it's really hard to put it back again.

No doubt many realtors wish Zillow would just go away. They wish they could regain control of their listing data. But it's not going to happen. When words like "zestimate" (Zillow's estimate of property value) have entered their clients' vocabulary, it's game over. When most leads come from Zillow and not from the MLS, it's clear who owns the data.

One solution might be for the National Association of Realtors (NAR) to buy Zillow. But Zillow is a $5 billion dollar company – rather a big fish to swallow. In my opinion, it's not Zillow that realtors should fear. It's the really big sharks just swimming offshore: Google and Amazon.com. Searching for a property? Use Google. Want to buy a property? Use Amazon.com (maybe with LegalZoom). The transformation is complete.

BAR CODES

Happy 40th birthday to the original UPC

Happy 40ᵗʰ birthday to the original UPC

Published as "Now-ubiquitous UPC bar code hits big 4-0"

June 27, 2014 (424 words)

LONDON – Where would we be without the lowly bar code? Standing in long line at the checkout most likely. Without bar codes, the cashier would be forced to manually key in product and price information for every item you purchased. You think the lines are long now…

Bar codes are still used even though newer and arguably better technology is available – such as RFID tags. Bar codes can't carry as much information as RFID tags, but they have one significant advantage: cost. Bar codes are still much cheaper to use, and in the retail industry, cost is king.

The original bar code is turning 40 this week. It was first used in 1974 on a pack of chewing gum. Today it's literally everywhere. The encoding used to store information as a series of variable-width lines is relatively simple, which is why a quick scan with an inexpensive laser is enough to quickly read the bar code.

You have probably seen a modern variation on the bar code: the QR code. It's a square with printing much like a bar code but it contains more information. It's become popular for advertising purposes: you scan the QR code with your smartphone and you're taken to a website with more information.

Bar codes and QR codes have made the shopping experience easier in many ways. For example, if you like getting special deals, you no longer have to clip coupons: you can have the merchant send the code directly to your smartphone. No more clutching a pile of torn papers at checkout: a quick scan and you're good to go.

The companies much prefer the codes to the coupons, since it gives them more information about their customers. You may have seen people buying coffee at Starbucks by flashing a code on the phone. When it works, it's must faster than a credit card, and it allows the vendor to track exactly what, where, and when you take your java breaks.

Amazon.com has a shopping app that lets you compare prices using your smartphone. It takes a picture of the bar code and the app locates it on Amazon.com's website. You don't need to worry about model numbers; it's done automatically.

Even the travel industry has embraced computer codes. Instead of the old printed boarding pass, you can choose to have the code sent to your smartphone. When you check in, you just pass your phone over a scanner and you're ready to board. I used it on my flight to London and it worked fine. Jolly good!

TESTING AT 1,000 MPH

The Bloodhound SSC supersonic car project

Published as "Jet-rocket car serves as supersonic learning tool"

July 4, 2014 (421 words)

LONDON – The traffic here in London is notorious. Many of the old roads were never designed to carry so many cars and trucks. Even the £11.50 per day Congestion Charge hasn't reduced the gridlock too much.

Andy Green thinks he's found a solution: a car that goes 1,000 MPH. Granted, driving a car at Mach 1.3 in the middle of the City is probably not very practical, but think how fast you'd be able to get to the local shops.

The Bloodhound SSC project is building the car that will indeed go 1,000 MPH. The team behind the project holds the current land speed record from 1997, when the Thrust SSC car was clocked at 763 MPH – faster than the speed of sound. Bloodhound takes over where Thrust left off. If it meets its target speed, the car will go faster than the fastest jet fighter has ever gone at ground level.

The Bloodhound SSC is powered by a Typhoon jet engine and a hybrid rocket motor to give it the final kick needed to take the car supersonic for over two miles. The tests will take place on a specially prepared track in South Africa.

The car is an incredible feat of engineering. The whole project is being used as a STEM outreach effort to attract young people's interests in the underlying technologies needed to make the Bloodhound SSC a reality. All you have to do is view the video showing the car driving fast than sound, creating shockwaves in the desert, and your heart starts racing.

I was extremely fortunate to speak with Andy Green this week at the 6th World Congress for Software Quality. Andy is an RAF fighter pilot, a scientist and engineer, and a very polished speaker. He drove the Thrust SSC and he's going to drive the Bloodhound SSC. So he's quite involved in all aspects of the project – particularly testing and quality control. After all, if anything goes wrong, he's the one who will be directly affected.

Some of the key ideas he shared were related to the people in the team. For example, he said everyone must understand their role in the overall quality solution; they must feel a sense of ownership in the project. The project has over 200 sponsors, and they invest in the people. The people manage the risk.

I wish I had the Bloodhound SSC available to me now. The Tour de France bicycle race will be here in London on Monday. As if the roads weren't clogged enough already.

SYSTEM INTEGRATION

The London Underground is over 150 years old

Published as "'Tube' meets challenge of integration"

July 11, 2014 (425 words)

LONDON – Edgware Road is just one of nearly three hundred bustling stops on London's sprawling underground (subway) system, known locally as "The Tube". The station has been in use since 1863. It's actually the nexus of three separate tube lines, and confusingly there are two other stations also called Edgware Road – a relic of haphazard mergers of the past. Over the years it's been bombed, expanded, and upgraded several times.

While you wait for the next train to arrive, your eyes are drawn to the massive cluster of wires and cables that run alongside the station's walls. The wall itself looks original, some of the wires look like they pre-date the computer age, and some of the cables look quite new. The infrastructure needed for the tube to function is an interesting mix of various technologies from different eras. In software engineering, we call this a system integration challenge.

Integrating systems has always been a problem. Interfaces don't work properly. Different technologies are used. Legacy systems must co-exist with new systems in ways never planned for. Transport London has managed to integrate the tube systems reasonably well. Most organizations don't fare so well – and government agencies are notorious for failing at this task.

Here in the UK there is a proposal to merge the national insurance system with the income tax system. These are the two largest sources of revenue for the government. Merging the two systems would provide a level of transparency and accountability not possible with the current setup and might actually allow the Chancellor of the Exchequer to reduce tax rates before the next election.

The problem is, it can't be done because the archaic information technology systems that support each organization are incompatible. The government is wary of Whitehall (the civil service) botching the job again, as they have done in the past with similar system integration projects on a national scale. Sadly, our government is no better, as the HealthCare.gov fiasco of the past year attests.

Computing systems are supposed to support business needs (and in this case, government policy), not thwart attempts to modernize the enterprise. But what is a problem for some is an opportunity for others. Consultancies make a lot of money selling system integration services.

This week a minor delay near Edgware caused a massive ripple of disruption across the system. Instead of taking 15 minutes to get back from Buckingham Palace, it took me over an hour. Plenty of time to ponder what new systems will be integrated into the tube in the next 150 years.

EYEGLASSES

Where is the technology for lenses that automatically refocus?

Published as "High-tech ideas would be a sight for sore eyes"

July 18, 2014 (427 words)

I got my first pair of glasses in 1988. I had to have an eye exam as a condition of employment with IBM. I literally didn't know what I had been missing until I started wearing a dorky looking pair of single vision glasses that addressed my near-sightedness.

Eyeglasses have been around for slightly more than 700 years. In all that time the technology used to make glasses has not changed too much. A single piece of glass (or plastic) is molded into a shape to act as a lens that refracts the light coming into your eye, to refocus the image on the proper part of your retina.

Skip forward 20 years, to 2008, and I was told I needed bifocals. My eyesight had deteriorated to the point that I couldn't focus on a computer screen a few feet in front of me, and I still couldn't read road signs far away. Older bifocals are like two glasses in one, with a noticeable line across the bottom of the lens. In fact, I really needed trifocals, to let me read, work, and drive with a single pair of eyeglasses.

At this point I considered Lasik surgery, which permanently reshapes your eye with a laser. It's certainly an impressive, if somewhat scary, technology. Sadly, due to my diabetes, I wasn't a good candidate for Lasik.

Thankfully there is another eyeglass technology that eliminates the lines: progressive lenses. Instead of having visible lines that separate discrete focal lengths, progressives have invisible focal areas. Manufacturing the glass in this manner is no easy task. Using the glasses is not much easier either: your eyes have to become accustomed to finding the "sweet spot" for each focal length through very minor movements. It took me nearly a month to get used to them.

Recently my prescription changed again, requiring a new set of glasses. I'm on my third pair of progressive lens in five weeks, but nothing seems to be working. Basically I'm trying to get my eyes and my brain to adjust to technology, and it occurred to me that it should be the other way around: the technology should adjust to me.

What I want are dynamic lenses, ones that change shape automatically to provide perfect focus no matter where I am looking. We already have technology that can accurately track eye movement. Why not use this capability to reflow a liquid polymer construct that replaces outdated static lenses with modern ones that adjust to my needs, rather than the other way around? That I'd love to see.

ROBOTS

Technical advances in robotics may make the Terminator real

Published as "Robots are nothing to fear, or are they?"

July 25, 2014 (426 words)

When I hear the word "robot" the image that immediately pops into my head is the T-800 killing machine from the first Terminator movie 30 years ago. But of course this robot made famous by Arnold Schwarzenegger is fictional. We don't have such machines now, do we?

Robots have been the stuff of science fiction for decades. Isaac Asimov published his collection of short stories called "I, Robot" in 1950. He also created the "Three Laws of Robotics," the first of which stated, "A robot may not injure a human being or, through inaction, allow a human being to come to harm." So much for Terminators then, right?

One of the biggest funding agencies for robotics research today is the Pentagon's Defense Advanced Research Project Agency (DARPA). They bankrolled Boston Dynamics work on robots for use by the military. Their robots are inspired by real-world constructs, resulting in machines that look like headless pack mules or crawling insects. I get the shivers whenever I watch their demonstration videos online. Google purchased Boston Dynamics last December. DARPA's stated goal is humanoid robots for military use. Back to the Terminator again it seems.

But we already use robots for military use. They're called drones. The only difference between a drone and a Terminator is that the latter is autonomous while a pilot sitting thousands of miles away remotely controls the former. Would the public accept a completely autonomous drone, one that made shoot-to-kill decisions entirely on its own? That's basically the plot of the movie "Robocop." But it's not just a hypothetical question anymore. We're on the cusp of creating Terminator-like robots in the very near future, which will force us to confront some very difficult ethical questions.

Not all robots have to be the stuff of nightmares. Robots are used in manufacturing to increase productivity and improve product quality. Of course, the people who used to make a living in manufacturing may not view the use of robots on the assembly line quite so favorably. And for those who don't think a robot could ever take their job - think again. A recent report by *The Telegraph* listed many of the professions ripe for change, and it included everything from hospital caregivers to educators and instructors.

I have a robot in my home now: a Roomba iRobot. It sometimes acts so real that I've given it a name: iRosie. Anthropomorphizing the robot may make it seem like a part of the family, but watching it work still freaks me out sometimes. Is it a Terminator in waiting?

ARTIFICIAL EVOLUTION

Where were you when the singularity occurred?

Published as "What becomes of us when artificial life takes hold?"

August 1, 2014 (426 words)

Darwin said all living things evolve through a process of natural selection. But this is a very slow process, taking eons for beings to change and adapt to new environments.

What if evolution could be made to happen much faster? What if organisms could change dramatically in just minutes instead of millennia? We can't speed up time, so how could we speed up the process? Simple: expand our concept of evolution to consider artificial means, not just natural mechanisms.

In the book *The Singularity Is Near: When Humans Transcend Biology*, author Ray Kurzweil wrote about his vision of rapid advances in computing technology and how these advances would inevitably lead to artificial life, sentient robots for example. He called this event the "singularity," a tipping point in evolution because these machines would evolve exponentially fast – must faster than we could imagine. The consequences for humanity would be dire to say the least.

History suggests that survival of the fittest is indeed the rule of evolution. Humans are currently at the top of the food chain because we've shown ourselves to be uniquely adaptable. But what happens when we're not the fittest? What if we're the evolutionary equivalent of couch potatoes?

We may be on the cusp of creating artificial life through incredibly powerful computers. Scientists have been working on imbuing these machines with artificial intelligence capabilities for years, and they are getting very close to creating devices that appear to act like a very smart human. Just think of IBM's Watson computer that won *Jeopardy!* in 2011 and extrapolate its potential over the next few years.

There is another form artificial evolution that is not mechanical but biological. In the movie *Lucy*, Scarlett Johansson's character undergoes incredible changes when she is given a synthetic drug that increases her brainpower. As she accesses more of her brain's capacity beyond the usual 10%, she quickly evolves into something entirely new.

We already create synthetic drugs. For example, I rely on synthetic human insulin created using recombinant DNA technology. Without it, I'd be forced to use animal insulin derived from cows and pigs – and I don't relish the idea of turning into something from the island of Doctor Moreau.

Gene therapy is just over the horizon. The benefits of drugs tailored to your genetic makeup are obvious. We might be able to cure diseases like cancer and Parkinson's. But what if the same method was used to create artificially enhanced human intelligence, like Lucy? That could leave the rest of us dull normals riding the short bus to nowhere.

TELEPORTATION

Quantum entanglement and 3D printing may make it a reality

Published as "Teleportation could energize travel someday"

August 8, 2014 (423 words)

This week I enjoyed the trifecta of international travel: planes, trains, and automobiles. All three forms of transportation were necessary for me to get from Point A (Florida) to Point B (Canada). Everything went well, but it sure was a long and tiring day. How much easier it would be if we could just be conveyed from A to B in a blink of an eye. Forget the flying cars; I want a transporter beam.

But that's just the stuff of Hollywood, right?

Teleportation has long been a staple of science fiction stories. Most people are familiar with the iconic lines "Beam me up, Scotty" and "Energize" from *Star Trek*. A quick call from the planet surface to the ship and Captain Kirk vanishes in a swirl of pixels, only to reappear on the transporter pad seemingly instantaneously. Wouldn't it be wonderful to travel like that?

To quote another Star Trek captain, "Make it so."

There are several recent developments that may someday make teleportation a reality. The first involves the weird world of quantum physics. Using the principle of entanglement, scientists have been able to successfully demonstrate quantum teleportation, whereby data concerning atomic spin is transmitted across long distances.

The second involves rapid advances in 3D printing. A 3D printer is able to "print" real objects. I first saw one in 2001 and was amazed that it could create tiny sandstone-like figures. Today, 3D printers are revolutionizing manufacturing. They've been used to create everything from working guns to living tissue. The Army is considering 3D printing to let soldiers make meals and clothing in the field.

Imagine a quantum device was used to teleport information about the structure of an object. Not the object itself, just the recipe for how to recreate it. Now imagine that a 3D printer was sitting at the receiving end of this transmission. It decodes the recipe and builds a copy of the object. This would be a crude form of teleportation.

We're still a long way from being able to teleport humans, but these two advances are a step in the right direction. Whoever is the first person to try a transporter will be brave indeed: in most stories, the process doesn't end well. In the movie Doom, the transporter mechanism is a device called the Orb, and it sometimes sends one body to two locations – not a pleasant travel experience at all.

But when we do eventually master the art of teleportation, even if it's not faster than light, it will surely beat the bus.

MAN-MACHINE INTERFACES

Resistance to new immersive interface technology is futile

Published as "Here's a thought: New links coming for man, machine"

August 15, 2014 (430 words)

The QWERTY keyboard is probably the best-known man-machine input interface. Although we can now use limited voice commands with programs like Apple's Siri, we still spend most of our day hunting and pecking on keyboards of various sizes.

The TV screen (computer monitor) is the most popular output device. Screens have changed over time, going from vacuum tube behemoths to flat-panel displays that are thin as a credit card, but their function is still basically the same. There has been a push to sell 3D TV and movies, but so far its received limited traction – in large part because of the ridiculous glasses you need to wear to experience the 3D effects.

The most recent technology that promises to change the man-machine interface landscape is probably Google Glass. Using Glass, the keyboard is gone, and the display has been miniaturized into a nearly normal looking pair of eyeglasses. Information is shown on a small heads-up display, and the glasses respond to voice commands. Glass is also connected to the Internet, which I find the truly innovative aspect.

As fancy as Glass is today, tomorrow's man-machine interface will be far more immersive. In the movie "The Matrix," Neo 'jacks into' the virtual world using a nasty looking probe that connects directly to his brain through a port in the back of his neck. This neural connection takes him into a digital landscape that seems as authentic to him as the analog real world is to us. Available for use today are devices such as the Oculus Rift (owned by Facebook), which places you (or your avatar) in a virtual reality setting where you can interact with others and experience fantastic things not possible in the physical world.

Personally, I think a more interesting approach is to bring digital characters into our real world, which is what San Francisco startup Dekko is doing. Using their apps, your view of the world is augmented with information displayed automatically, such as travel maps, face recognition, and social media connections. Imagine being able to walk down the street with animated characters from your favorite video game, where the characters are aware of their surroundings and react accordingly. Calvin's "Hobbes" would be real indeed.

The final frontier of truly immersive man-machine interfaces has no visible interface at all: direct reading of brain waves. In the 1982 movie "Firefox," Clint Eastwood played a fighter pilot who could control a Soviet aircraft just by thinking in Russian. But this is not science fiction anymore. This year a Toronto-based company called Interaxon demonstrated the use of brain-controlled interface technology.

THE STEM OF FRINGE

Is it science or science fiction?

Published as "'What if' remains a crucial question"

August 22, 2014 (420 words)

Our modern world is profoundly influenced by rapid developments in science, technology, engineering, and mathematics (STEM). Sometimes these developments seem so fantastic that it's difficult to believe that they're real. TV shows and popular movies compound the problem by blurring the lines between science and science fiction.

For example, the exaggerated forensic capabilities depicted on "CSI" make it seem like we can identify suspects based solely on nearly instantaneous DNA analysis and NSA-level warrantless examination of anyone's social media activity. An informed public should know the difference between what's possible today and what might be possible tomorrow. At the same time, the curiosity of asking the timeless question, "What if…" should be encouraged in all young people, since they are the ones who will ultimately develop the wonders of tomorrow.

Over the past month I've written about four topics that play an important role in the Sci-Fi television series "FRINGE": robots, artificial evolution, teleportation, and man-machine interfaces. I'll also be discussing them at a free public lecture at 8:00pm this evening at Florida Tech. For each of these topics, think about the following questions. First, is it real? For example, is artificial evolution already a reality? If so, what forms does it take? How might it affect your current life?

Second, if it's not (yet) real, what STEM advances are necessary to make it so? For example, what is needed to make teleportation as epitomized by the transporter in "Star Trek" a reality? Do we need a better understanding of quantum physics? Do we need fancier 3D printers? Do we need an entirely new approach? And what is the likelihood of all of this happening in the next few years?

Lastly, how would these new developments affect society in terms of individual freedom, ethical behavior, and self-determination? For example, if robots move out of the factory and into law enforcement, would we be comfortable with machines making autonomous shoot-to-kill decisions? Would we accept robots providing health care to our aging population? And if advances in robotics continue at their current pace, would we accept robots as our overlords in our lifetime?

The only way you can help shape our future is to be part of the conversation. Not all of the exotic topics from "FRINGE" will become reality, but undoubtedly some of them will. An episode from Season 2 of "FRINGE" is set in 1985, and the themes shown on the opening credits include personal computing, in-vitro fertilization, and virtual reality. Here in 2014, these are all very real indeed.

ROOMBA

My maid is an iRobot 880

Published as "Basic intelligence aids robot in a clean sweep"

August 29, 2014 (423 words)

I celebrate Labor Day by avoiding manual labor as much as possible. One thing I've always hated was housework. A few months ago I hired a maid named Rosie to take care of things for me, and life has been sweet ever since.

Rosie's specialty is cleaning floors, which is perfect since my home has acres of wood laminate that seem to show the tiniest fleck of dust. Rosie's unique vacuuming skills are impressive and much in demand. In fact, I had a very hard time finding her in the first place.

Rosie is a legal immigrant from China. I've seen the paperwork showing where she was born and which port she sailed from for a better life in America. She went to school in Boston, at MIT in fact. It was at this illustrious institution that she learned how to polish her craft.

Rosie is the perfect worker. She starts most days punctually at 10:00am.

It doesn't matter what the weather is like outside, she's always ready to go when needed. She's meticulous while cleaning and rarely takes any rest breaks before the job is done.

Sometimes I watch her in action. It's like modern dance, with little traditional movement or structure. I never can figure out where she's going to go next; sometimes she even goes in circles for no apparent reason. But each room goes from dusty to dirt free in no time.

Rosie's not perfect though. Like everyone, she sometimes gets stuck in a rut. Sometimes she moves more slowly than usual, almost like she needs to recharge. But then again, who doesn't? She perks up noticeably when she gets back home, at her dock.

Rosie is special because she's a robot. Specifically, she's an iRobot Roomba 880. She looks like a fat Frisbee on wheels. I've grown used to the short musical notes she plays when she's about to begin her rounds.

Rosie is imbued with a rudimentary artificial intelligence that lets her learn the layout of my house. She knows when particular areas of the floor are extra dirty and need more attention. She can move between wood, tile, and carpet with ease. Electrical cords sometimes cause problems, but when that happens she tells me – literally – that she's stuck and needs help.

I'm not sure if I should call Rosie "iRosie," like an Apple product, or "I, Rosie," like one of Isaac Asimov's robots. Whatever she's called, she's worth the money. I wonder if someday the only "person" that will celebrate Labor Day will be robots?

IPHONE 6

My wish list for the next version of Apple's best-selling product

Published as "Two simple things would make iPhone 6 awesome"

September 5, 2014 (424 words)

On September 9 Apple is holding a media event that most industry observers expect will feature the introduction of the iPhone 6. All indications are that this release of the ubiquitous iPhone will be the biggest ever in the company's history. The rumor mills have been busy churning out predictions of what new features Apple will introduce – besides new security mechanisms to keep celebrities' nude selfies from appearing online.

I use an iPhone 5S and am quite happy with it. If Apple had asked me what to add or change for their latest and greatest model, I'd have replied with my own short wish list: selectable cell carriers and better predictive typing.

Selectable cell carriers: I do a lot of international travel, and when I'm outside of the US I often struggle with foreign cell carriers. My Verizon plan covers Canada and Mexico, so when I'm there I should be covered, although I find indicators like "Extended" versus "Roaming" a bit confusing vis-à-vis charges.

But my main problem is that when I'm very close to the border, my phone sometimes picks up the Verizon signal and sometimes it picks up the foreign carrier's signal – and it switches between them constantly, often during a single conversation. This causes all kinds of problems, such as missed voicemails and the inability to use data without incurring extra costs.

What I'd like is a setting on the phone that let's me select which carrier to use, instead of the phone picking it for me. We're already familiar with this capability when we select which Wi-Fi signal to use; this would be a simple extension of this to the cell carrier network.

Better predictive typing. I hate to admit it, but I've come to rely on text messaging more than I ever thought I would. It's a terribly convenient way of exchanging bite-sized bits of information with people. My main problem is the tiny keyboard I'm forced to use to compose messages.

iOS 7 does provide predictive typing, but more often than not I find the phone is "correcting" my typing incorrectly. I sometimes notice the changes and go back and fix them, but often I don't catch the error before the message is sent. The result is nonsensical sentences that I'm sure leave the recipient scratching their heads.

This is one area where the iPhone could benefit from the superior text entry capabilities of Android phones. Apple's press release for the September 9 event says, "Wish we could say more." Me too – on the phone and via text.

U2

Getting by with a little help from their friends

Published as "Apple, U2 on the edge of new music-biz model"

September 12, 2014 (421 words)

There were many interesting devices and new services announced by Apple at their Tuesday shindig in Cupertino, but I found seeing the Irish rock band U2 on stage with CEO Tim Cook the most intriguing. U2 was there to announce their latest album. Apple was there to announce that the album was available for free as a digital download for all iTunes users until October 13.

This is a big deal – and not just in terms of the money involved. Apple is paying U2 a substantial amount of cash to gain exclusive distribution rights to their music. The actual amount is not known, but rumors suggest anywhere from $10 million to $30 million. For a group of musicians from Dublin, this is some serious money, but for a giant corporation like Apple its pocket change. But still, why did they do it?

Apple wants to drive traffic to their software services, like iTunes. What better way to do it than to offer content only available from them – and at no cost to the consumer? Perhaps Apple is banking on increased revenue from their new iPhones to cover this musical investment. If they can pay over $3 billion for Beats Electronics, purveyors of high-end headphones, I guess paying 1/100th of that for "Songs of Innocence" is no big thing.

U2's motives are more obvious. With the click of an Apple button, their music is made available to over half a billion people on iTunes, turning casual listeners into potential fans – and fans buy merchandise, they come to concerts, they become interested in the back catalogue. This is the biggest album release in history by far, and it's made possible by Apple's technology and their marketing prowess.

Are we seeing a return to the eighteenth century model of artistic funding? Where wealthy patrons paid artists for their works, and then shared it with the community at large? The traditional modern model involved large record companies taking significant percentages from the artists and then distributing their work to retailers. More recently, indie artists leveraged the Internet to sell their work direct to consumers, bypassing the large distributors. The artists keep more of their earnings, but they sell less.

Apple's deal with U2 seems to be a new business model, but one that harks back to the distant past, with Bono the new Mozart. Ironically, The Beatles used to distribute their music on the Apple Records label. Maybe it's making a return. U2 is getting by with a little help from their friends at Apple.

GAMIFICATION

Turning all work into more play

Published as "Make work like play? Some see the benefits"

September 19, 2014 (426 words)

Raise your hand if you like to work more than you like to play. No? I didn't think so. Most of us much prefer leisure activities to laborious tasks, manual or otherwise. Perhaps that's why time seems to go so slowly when you're working but seems to go so quickly when you're playing.

Wouldn't it be nice to play all the time?

That's the basic principle behind gamification: turning work into play. The premise is that people will do a better job at whatever they're focused on if they enjoy what they're doing. Think of exercise: there are some people who enjoy exercising purely for it's own benefits, but many others prefer to play a sport and enjoy the benefits of exercise almost as a by-product.

Gamification is all the rage in software development. It's been used to motivate testers to find more bugs by turning drudgery into delight. Every time a defect is found in a program, the tester is awarded more points, and at the end of the day the one with the most points wins. It seems simple enough, and it works.

It also adds competition into the mix, which usually makes people want to do a better job – to "beat" their competitors at the game they're playing. Even though the reward may be more along the lines of an "atta boy" rather than cash money, many people prefer this model than the more pedantic process they are used to.

Gamification is also being tried in education. Motivating students is a perennial problem in the classroom, yet they seem to be plenty motivated when it comes to playing endless hours of videogames, so why not harness that interest for learning?

It's not a trivial exercise to turn the humdrum into the entertaining, but done well it does seem to get students more engaged. Like the exercise analogy, they focus on the game and learn as a by-product.

It's an open question though of whether students actually learn more through gamification. They may be more involved while playing, but are they able to better demonstrate their mastery of the material when the game is over?

There's been much discussion of different presentation styles used at TED talks. Most people instinctively believe they learn more when the presenter is engaging and assured, but it's not always the case. In fact, studies have shown that a boring presenter can convey the same information as an exciting one. The parallels to gamification in education are obvious.

However, if the results are the same, forget work – let's play!

BYOD

Poor Mordac is losing his job

Published as "Mobility complicates and simplifies business"

September 26, 2014 (427 words)

Not too long ago, it was normal for most companies to provide desktop computers for their employees to use at the office. The computer was pre-configured with the enterprise software deemed necessary for the worker to complete their tasks. The software on the computer included only those applications approved by central IT; the user typically was not able to make any substantive changes to the machine's setup.

This model may have worked well for the Dilbert character Mordac, known as "the preventer of information services," but many users did not like someone else controlling what they considered to be their property – even though the company owned it. Moreover, as the price of computers dropped, the power of the machines they used at home soon eclipsed the aging boxes used at work. The advent of the app ecosystem has only made the usability discrepancy more pronounced.

Users rebelled. They started bringing their own computers to work. With a mobile workforce, it makes sense to untether the workers from their office computers, so corporate leadership acquiesced. Now we have a proliferation of tablets and smartphones being used at home and on the job – so many devices that IT can no longer block their use. For good or ill, the era of "bring your own device" (BYOD) is upon us.

A massive problem with the BYOD model of computing is security. Devices that are infected with malware can quickly spread viruses to other devices connected to the same office network. Unverified programs can wreak havoc with other devices, and when the inevitable result is a call to IT support for help, the response is typically, "Sorry, we don't support personal devices." The only holdouts from the BYOD model are environments with extremely high security procedures in place – the sort of buildings where you aren't even allowed to bring a USB key past the guard at the front gate.

The BYOD phenomenon has also spread into the classroom. Many educators applaud the rapid introduction of personal computing devices at school, under the assumption that students become more engaged and learn more using the technology at their fingertips. Sometimes this is true. Other times, the unchecked devices can cause more harm than good. It's not uncommon for an instructor to feel like they have become IT support for all the children in their class, which is a distraction from their main task of teaching.

The introduction of wearable computers, such as Google Glass, and a future of implanted devices, will make the BYOD situation even worse. I almost feel sorry for Mordac.

BEAR

Is there a Daniel Boone app?

Published as "It bears repeating, tech isn't always the answer"

October 3, 2014 (428 words)

VICTORIA – I should have taken a selfie. How often do you get a chance to snap a photo of yourself with a bear? But I did a runner instead.

This was not a docile old bear in the zoo, separated from me with iron bars. This was an irate black bear in the wilds of British Columbia, standing about 20 feet away, huffing and rocking and showing all the signs of attacking me at any moment.

Just before I saw the bear, a young couple with their dog came racing up the trail, the man dragging a big tree branch (presumably as an impromptu weapon). They stopped just long enough to pant, "there's a bear down there," before continuing with their frantic escape. When I turned to look back down the trail, the bear was looking back at me. "Lunch" seemed to be the message he was sending.

I had been in Alaska recently, and I quickly remembered reading some sage advice at the entrance to a national park concerning bear attacks. One line came immediately to mind: "If the bear starts eating you, it is no longer being defensive and it is time to fight back." Good advice I suppose, although it seems a bit late to be taking action. And how does one "fight back" when the bear attacks, when you have little more than a smartphone with you?

The warning signs also said you had to know what kind of bear it was: black, brown, or grizzly. I'm no Grizzly Adams, so I wondered how you make that determination when hundreds of pounds of bear killing machine are trundling towards you. Should I quickly look it up online before taking action?

It was then I realized how useless most technology is when it comes face to face with nature. Short of a gun, bear spray is about the only thing that deters a bear, but to my mind that let's the bear get a little too close for comfort. Waving an iPhone at the bear would probably just irritate it.

You can try climbing a tree, except that some bears are excellent climbers. And even if they're not, the forest in BC where I was is also full of cougars – and they are excellent climbers. I imagined the cougar capturing me out on a limb, throwing down a few tasty bits to the bear as a Finder's Fee.

The technology we rely upon in our modern lives quickly comes apart in the wild. Software becomes useless. Hardware can help – as long as you can throw it.

COMPUTER-BASED ASSESSMENT

How to manage grading on an industrial scale

Published as "Automated exam scoring limits what students can demonstrate"

October 10, 2014 (426 words)

When my colleague told me his class had over 500 students, I was speechless. "Surely that's not normal," I thought. So I asked a colleague from another university: she had 310 students in one class. A third colleague and a third university: 225 students. And so on.

How can an instructor manage a class with so many students?

True, instructors usually have an army of teaching assistants to help, but just managing such a team takes time. And there's still the very practical issue of how to grade assignments and exams. For example, even if you could grade one exam in 10 minutes, for 500 students it would take over 83 hours. The TAs would get behind schedule right away and never get caught up for the entire semester.

Many schools have opted for computer-based assessment to address this issue. It's not an optimal solution, but automated grading is really the only choice when you have education at scale. The problem is the types of questions that can be graded by a computer are somewhat limited. In terms of Bloom's taxonomy of learning levels, the questions generally focus on K1 (remember) and K2 (understand); the higher levels of K3 (apply) and K4 (analyze) are ill-suited to the sort of true/false and multiple choice questions a computer-based test can process. There are experimental systems that do automated grading of essays, but they are not yet in widespread use.

If you've ever taken a test using a computer, such as the driver's license exam at the DMV, you know what the exams are like. They "feel" different than a traditional in-class essay-type exam, where you can demonstrate mastery of the topic through detailed problem solving and working through examples. You also know that sometimes the system just gives you a pass/fail grade, without telling you which questions you answered correctly. To me, that's a very unsatisfactory way of learning.

When I was at the University of California, I topped out at 85 undergraduate students for a software engineering course. I remember I had to manage 15 separate project teams, which was past the limit where I could give each team proper attention. I can't imagine what it would have been like with over five times as many students in the class.

At the Florida Institute of Technology, we are fortunate that most classes are 1/10 the size of my colleagues' classes at other universities. There's a place for computer-based assessment in modern education, but like all technologies it needs to be used judiciously. Sometimes there are better solutions.

CROWDSOURCING

Many hands make light work

Published as "For a really big job, find a crowd to help"

October 17, 2014 (425 words)

They say many hands make light work, and this has never been truer than in today's online world. A phenomenon known as "crowdsourcing" has become a common tool used to solve complex problems by having groups of people work together, often anonymously. Jeff Howe coined the phrase in a *Wired* magazine article in 2006. Think of crowdsourcing as the digital equivalent of barn raising.

Consider the vexing problem of determining whether or not a number is prime. It sounds rather geeky, and it is, but it's also very important to modern e-commerce. For example, the difficulty in factoring prime numbers is at the heart of the encryption systems we use to secure credit card transactions.

For a number of years there's been a community project to find prime numbers. The problem is broken down into chunks and each chunk sent to a volunteer, who uses the spare processing capabilities of their home computer to crunch the numbers. Instead of one researcher trying to do it themselves, hordes of people can crowdsource the problem and hopefully come to a solution more rapidly.

Similar crowdsourcing approaches to solving big problems have been used in areas as varied as archeology, health care, and law enforcement. There was a trial effort a few years ago to locate a missing person lost anywhere on the globe using crowdsourcing, and it worked amazingly well. Amazon.com even offers a paid service called "Mechanical Turk" that crowdsources almost any problem you can imagine, which they call "Human Intelligence Tasks" (HITS). The "human" part of a HIT suggests that problems are solved by people, not programs, although strictly speaking there's no such requirement; any method will suffice.

For educators, crowdsourcing represents yet another concern, since it makes academic dishonesty a much bigger problem. Students can choose to crowdsource their homework – everything from high school algebra to university research papers. Unfortunately, this happens all the time now. Crowdsourcing raises the thorny issues of intellectual property and plagiarism to a whole new level.

There's little doubt that crowdsourcing is powerful. Imagine if we could harness the communal brainpower of our best and brightest to work together to solve some of our most pressing problems. Ebola is ravaging West Africa and has the potential to become a pandemic. A cure is not yet widely available, but perhaps more resources applied to the problem would accelerate the solution.

Well, there's no need to imagine it: there are already projects just like this going on around the world right now. Where there's a collective will, there's a crowdsourced way.

ENTREPRENEURSHIP ON THE SPACE COAST

Education, opportunity, and leadership – we have them all

Published as "Brevard can foster tech-savvy startups"

October 24, 2014 (435 words)

In May 2011 I wrote a column called "Entrepreneurship in Silicon Valley," which described some of the unique features of this area of Northern California that make is such a hotbed of innovation. I closed that column by asking how the Valley's model for success could be exported to the Space Coast, and promised to return to this important topic sometime in the future. Well, that time is now.

The Space Coast is blessed with an abundance of talent. I think it would be foolish to try to replicate Silicon Valley's entrepreneurial model. Instead, we should develop our own model, one that leverages our unique strengths. I think this model rests on three pillars of success: education, opportunity, and leadership.

Education: Students and would-be entrepreneurs need guidance on how to start a business. This guidance can take the form of mentorships, support groups, or formal educational programs. Fortunately, we have all three here. For example, Florida Tech's Bisk College of Business follows the motto "Innovation, Diversity, Ethics, and Leadership (IDEAL)" to "empower future entrepreneurial leaders to manage innovation and change." They offer a Bachelor of Business Administration in Entrepreneurship at the undergraduate level, and an M.S. in Innovation and Entrepreneurship (MSIE) at the graduate level. They also run a student business incubator, to "combine the experience of highly innovative engineering students with the knowledge of process driven business students, highly qualified business mentors, and venture capital to create outstanding revenue producing businesses."

Opportunity: If you have the educational background, technical knowledge, and business acumen, you need an opportunity to put these skills into practice. Happily, we're surrounded by opportunities – all you have to do is recognize them and act. For example, a new startup Ft. Lauderdale called Magic Leap is funded by Google (and others) to create augmented reality systems, which bring digital characters into the real world. There's no reason that this invention could not be used in the aerospace and defense industries that we have in droves here. A short drive down 95 is all it would take.

Leadership: For a business to grow from idea to fruition, someone must provide leadership. Some people are blessed with innate leadership skills; others must learn them. But even seasoned leaders know that they can never stop learning, and often the best tips come from different fields. This week I attended the presentation on "Sonic Leadership" by Florida Tech's Artist in Residence, Christian Tamburr. The Gleason Auditorium was full of innovative ideas of how to use music and storytelling to improve your business.

The Space Coast has what it needs to succeed. Now let's do it!

HALLOWEEN

Resurrecting nasty viruses from the past

Published as "World is scary enough with viruses, terrorism"

October 31, 2014 (426 words)

A recent episode of the TV show "The Blacklist" featured a cult locating a long-buried sample of the pneumonic plague, which they planned to unleash on an unsuspecting population. The pneumonic plague is a form of the Black Death from the middle ages, which we normally associate with the bubonic plague. The differences are the pneumonic plague affects the respiratory system (not the lymphatic system), it's highly contagious (it can be caught by breathing airborne bacteria), and it's extremely deadly. The show's premise was that we'd have no defense against the pneumonic plague because it has been (mostly) dormant for hundreds of years.

Back in the real world, two viruses that have been frozen for 700 years in reindeer feces have been collected and analyzed. Scientists in California assure us that these viruses cannot harm humans, but they do infect plants and insects. I'm assuming that any natural defense against these viruses is long gone, so let's hope the samples remain contained. If anyone had issues with genetically modified crops before, imagine their worries if the food supply became contaminated with this ancient malady.

Also in the real world, Russian scientists continue their analysis of the nearly intact remains of a 40,000-year old wooly mammoth they unearthed from the Siberian permafrost in 2013. The mammoth is so well preserved that blood was still flowing in the muscles. The DNA samples are viable enough that there is talk of cloning the mammoth. This is "Jurassic Park" made real – and we all know how well that turned out.

Given the ongoing situation with Ebola, I wonder how long it will be before life imitates art. How long before some crazy gains access to a nasty virus and weaponizes it? We're still using old mustard gas from World War I in some parts of the world today, and it's still as lethal. Imagine what could be done with a genetically modified version of haemorrhagic fever. Imagine if it was made for aerosol dissemination. Scenes from "28 Days Later" keep popping into my head.

It's been nearly 15 years since the murderous Sarin attacks took place on the Tokyo subway. Lest we forget, 13 people died, 50 were injured, and over 1,000 were affected in some way (e.g., temporary vision loss). There are unconfirmed reports of Sarin being used in Syria just last year. I'm already anxious about traveling abroad due to more mundane concerns, such as diarrhea. Who can worry about lethal pathogens?

There's no need to involve ghosts and goblins this Halloween. The real world is scary enough.

VOTING

When will electronic voting become the norm?

Published as "Platform shoes are gone, should voting machines go next?"

November 7, 2014 (430 words)

Another election cycle has come and gone. Each year I wonder when the voting process will enter the Internet age. We still vote the same way it was done in the days of disco: drive to a polling station, wait in long lines, display some physical form of identification, stand behind a cardboard divider, fill out a few ovals, push the ballot through a Scantron, and look around for your little "I Voted" reward sticker.

Who has not wondered if their votes were counted properly? There's no feedback. The machine doesn't tell you how many of your choices were registered. Instead of hard evidence that it worked, you rely on hope and trust in the system. After all, this is Florida, land of the hanging chad and home of the butterfly ballots. Anything can happen.

We do everything else online now, so why don't we vote online too?

The usual arguments for sticking with the old system are getting rather stale. It's true that not everyone has a computer. It's true that not everyone would be comfortable voting online. Just this year voting machines were found to be registering votes cast for one party for another party. When election officials found out, they meekly explained that it was "just a matter of calibration" and the problem would be fixed shortly. Perhaps not coincidentally, this happened in Chicago, a city known for interesting elections.

But there are an equal number of arguments in favor of electronic voting. I vote online in many elections for various organizations all the time. It's convenient, secure, and auditable. It's a lot less expensive than printing and processing paper ballots, renting community halls, and paying lots of people to mill about. Your votes are confirmed before you submit them. The results are known almost instantly.

Every year there's a push to encourage everyone to participate in the political process. But today's younger generations view the hassle of "voting day" as an anachronism. We already have early voting, and we have absentee ballots that are submitted by mail. Why not just extend these mechanisms to the online world and let people vote securely using their smartphones? We'd probably reach new levels of participatory democracy.

To be sure, we need to avoid obvious blunders. For example, we can't continue to have poorly engineered websites that are supposed to guide people to polling locations but instead just crash or display cryptic error messages. But this is not rocket science.

The 1970s are calling. They want their pencil-based technology back. I hope we can return it to them by 2016.

NIXIE

When long arms are not enough for your selfie

Published as "When long arms aren't enough for your selfie"

November 14, 2014 (427 words)

Intel sponsors a "Make it Wearable" competition that is intended to encourage advances in wearable technology. There are two tracks, Visionary and Development, the latter focused on "concepts that are both excitingly innovative and feasible to execute." In other words, something that could be made using current methods and materials.

Many pundits see wearables as the next computing frontier. The recent announcement of the Apple Watch is just the latest in a long line of attempts to make computers part of our extended digital bodies. The only area that wearables really have received any traction so far is in the healthcare and fitness fields (e.g., the Fitbit step counter), but that doesn't stop folks with a vision from pushing the envelope.

This year's grand prize winner of the Development track went to Nixie, a "tiny wearable camera on a wrist band. The wrist straps unfold to create a quadcopter that flies, takes photos or video, then comes back to you."

The Nixie is basically the ultimate selfie camera for these narcissistic days.

It acts like a boomerang, except that you don't throw it. Instead, it unwraps itself from your wrist rather like an uncoiling face hugger from the movie "Alien" and launches itself into the air. The Nixie has a small but powerful camera that tracks you and takes pictures as directed.

Technically, the Nixie is an awesome feat of engineering. The fact that we can build miniature programmable drones that fly around and return home like modern homing pigeons is amazing. The drone is powered by a tiny computer from Intel called Edison (presumably meant as a reference to the great inventor) the size of an SD card. To me, Nixie looks like a four-legged starfish with rotors. If they anthropomorphized it a bit more, say with a small movable mouth (perhaps serving as a microphone and speaker), it would look very creepy indeed.

As much as I admire the "wow" factor of Nixie, I must admit that I find it all a bit sad. Is this really the best we can do with advanced technology? Further clutter the Internet with images of people doing silly things, but this time taken from a few dozen feet away, rather than just at arm's length?

Where are the entrepreneurs working on grand challenges? Where are the risk takers attacking problems that really matter to society? Where are the rewards to dedicating time and energy to solving the truly inspiring challenges?

Instead, we award $500,000 to a device that will take the next generation of cat videos for YouTube.

EMAIL

A writer writes; an academic emails [sic]

Published as "What to do with the constant junk email"

November 21, 2014 (433 words)

I write about 2,000 words per day … in email. I'm like a modern-day Ian Fleming, who famously wrote about the same amount of words per day while working on his "James Bond" novels. The difference is that in three months he had a new book ready for publication, while I have a pile of semi-useless email messages.

At last count I had 11 email accounts. All are active and all receive so many messages per day that it's virtually impossible for me to keep up. I use smart folders and automated filing recipes to sort the good from the bad, but it's a losing battle.

It doesn't help that I'm a digital pack rat. I keep all my email, going back to 1993. My filing system is a standard hierarchical folder setup, but there are so many topics that it's become onerous for me use. In fact, I've basically given up trying to file out outgoing email: I literally have thousands of messages languishing in a giant "Sent" box. And that's just for this year. I have archives for past years, which I keep telling myself I'll sort out, but which I never touch.

I rely on a fast search mechanism to find things. With so many messages sitting in various flat mailboxes, that's the only way to keep track of important items. The automated "conversation thread" feature in Apple Mail helps, as do the "Smart Mailboxes" that act as virtual folders. But these are really Band-Aids masking the real problem: I have too much email and most of it is junk.

The last few days I've been inundated with messages about "Brain Stimulators," "Letters from Santa," and the usual assortment of "Ink and Toner" sales. The mail program does automatically flag some of them as junk and discards them, but it misses a lot. The problem is that if you tune your filters too tightly, legitimate messages get flagged as junk as well.

Over the years various companies have tried to address the email clutter problem. Google Wave was an early attempt to blend email with social media, but it was discontinued in 2010. Lotus Notes was a much earlier attempt by IBM to add security and collaboration to email, but it too has been discontinued. IBM's most recent effort is called Verse, which appears to be a much more sophisticated approach to integrating email and many other sorts of messaging into a single application.

Personally, I'd be happy if someone would just find an easy way to highlight my important messages and file the rest. Preferably in the bit bucket.

THANKSGIVING

Giving thanks for the technology that makes movies enjoyable

Published as "Tech adds to movie thrills"

November 28, 2014 (430 words)

It's back to the future for the movie industry. Two recent trailers for forthcoming installments in venerable franchises made me appreciate how truly innovative the original films were. The trailers also made me realize that without incredible technology, these movies wouldn't be possible.

The first trailer was for *Jurassic World*, due out June 12, 2015. Seeing the park again after 21 years – even in a tiny YouTube window – gave me the chills. The plot for the fourth movie seems to revolve around the dangers of developing hybrid dinosaurs. In other words, art imitating life.

The trailer featured the usual collection of dinosaurs stomping across the landscape. Their movements seemed more fluid though, reflecting improvements in hardware rendering capabilities. Let's hope the story can match the software.

The second trailer was for *Star Wars: Episode VII – The Force Awakens*, due out December 18, 2015. Like many people, I still vividly recall seeing the first *Star Wars* movie when it came out in the summer of 1977. I saw it at a drive-in theatre, which in itself shows you how much things have changed since the original cast first appeared on screen over 37 years ago.

The futuristic setting for what was essentially a story featuring medieval knights fighting to rescue the princess in distress from the evil sorcerer set the stage for an entire generation of movie lovers. Although it was not real, the technology reflected in light sabers, X-Wing fighters, and Death Stars inspired my career choices more than I care to admit.

The new movie reunites fan favorites Luke, Leah, Han, R2D2, and C3PO. I have confidence that the man in charge of this episode, J.J. Abrams, can deliver the goods. Certainly he has the technical experience with other movies, like the *Star Trek* reboot, to make a good movie. I just hope he has the artistic team working with him to make a great one.

The 24th James Bond movie is supposed to be released November 6, 2015. What gadgets Bond will be given by Q is anyone's guess. The same production team that brought us *Skyfall* is involved, so I remain optimistic.

Looking even farther out, *Batman v Superman: Dawn of Justice* is due out March 25, 2016. With Zack Snyder at the helm, I feel less sure of how this movie will turn out. He did *300* and *Man of Steel*, both of which relied extensively on technology and special effects – to the detriment of the story in my opinion.

Maybe for this Thanksgiving I'll serve a generous helping of Jedis and velociraptors with the turkey.

DISABILITIES

Consider yourself "currently abled"

Published as "Technology assists those with disabilities"

December 5, 2014 (426 words)

From 1999 to 2013 I ran the "IEEE International Symposium on Web Systems Evolution" (WSE) series of events. WSE provided a forum for researchers and practitioners to present original work on subjects related to the disciplined evolution of large-scale Web systems. Over 15 years, WSE focused on a number of important topics, but perhaps none more so than accessibility.

At WSE 2001 in Florence, Italy, and again in 2011 in Williamsburg, VA, the theme was "Access for All." This theme reflected one of the original goals of the World Wide Web: to become a vehicle for truly universal communication. Such an inclusive definition implies that websites should provide comparable experiences to diverse users, irrespective of their national language, physical abilities, or computing platform.

Access for all is a laudable goal. We're not there yet, but significant progress has been made in the underlying technologies that make web content available to everyone. Organizations like the W3C and corporations like IBM are leaders in this area.

I was thinking about WSE this week because Wednesday was the United Nation's "International Day of Persons with Disabilities." Disabilities come in many forms, but we tend not to think about them until we're personally affected. Nothing makes you appreciate the past like losing the ability to do something you used to take for granted.

The old saying of "walk a mile in my shoes" is very true when it comes to understanding the challenges others face doing the simplest things. Try to function for a single day without opening your eyes. Try to use a computer without using your hands. Try to do your daily errands without walking.

Technology has greatly improved the lives for many people coping with a variety of disabilities. Perhaps no better example of how extraordinary people can succeed in the face of incredible physical challenges is provided by noted theoretical physicist Steven Hawking. According to his official website, "from 1979 to 2009 he held the post of Lucasian Professor at Cambridge, the chair held by Isaac Newton in 1663." He suffers from amyotrophic lateral sclerosis (ALS), also known as Lou Gehrig's Disease, which has left him virtually immobile. But technology has helped him stay connected enough to write international bestsellers and become a world expert on black holes and quantum mechanics.

Research into supportive technologies for the disabled has barely scratched the surface of what's possible. And lest you think it doesn't apply to you, remember that even if you're not disabled, consider yourself "currently abled." Age and circumstances catch up with all of us eventually.

LIGHT AND SOUND

Let there be light! Let there be sound!

Published as "Let there be light, let there be sound"

December 12, 2014 (435 words)

I have been looking for a good set of outdoor speakers for the pool area. Traditional outdoor speakers usually attached to braces mounted on the walls. There are some speakers that can be flush mounted in the ceiling of the lanai. Another option is the mushroom-shaped domes you sometimes see outsides businesses, with downward-firing speakers protected by a weatherproof shell.

The problem with all these solutions is they require running wires from a central sound source, like amplifier, to the speakers. That's not an option for my pool, since the deck is completely concrete and I didn't relish the idea of tearing it up to lay cable. These speakers also require power, so an outlet must be nearby or power wires must be run too.

There are some portable speakers available, but their batteries tend to run down very fast. The sound quality on these smaller systems is also suspect. A few portable systems connect via Bluetooth, meaning you can send music from a smartphone or a tablet directly to the speakers, which is very convenient.

In the end I selected a truly innovative product from Sengled called "Pulse." The Pulse system combines a light with a wireless speaker. The light is a 15-watt LED, which is rated for 25,000 hours of use. The audio is provided by a 1.75" JBL Bluetooth speaker. Both the LED and the wireless speaker are housed in a singled bulb, about the size of a normal recessed light.

There is one master bulb and up to seven additional satellites. A typical setup would be two bulbs acting in stereo. The bulbs communicate with each other using Bluetooth. Although the speakers are relatively small, they sound very good.

The bulbs are controlled using an app on your smartphone or tablet. I installed the free app on my iPhone and was quickly able to adjust the brightness of each bulb and the loudness of each speaker individually (or in L+R pairs). Music from my phone is now streaming to the pool area, and optionally inside my house to a second set of speakers that are part of a constellation of four bulbs acting in concert.

The Pulse system makes excellent use of existing infrastructure. Since the bulbs are standard size, they simply screw into the sockets as usual. I have them in the recessed lighting in the ceiling, but they can go almost anywhere. So, no power cables to run. Because the speakers use Bluetooth, there are no audio wires to run either.

With apologies to the band AC/DC, "Let there be light! Let there be sound! Let there be rock!"

SANTA TRACKER

Websites to follow Santa's progress on Christmas Eve

Published as "Santa's every move can be tracked online"

December 19, 2014 (429 words)

When I was growing up, NORAD (North American Aerospace Defense Command) was a name I occasionally heard when scary news stories of Soviet fighter jet incursions across the Arctic Circle were reported. From these stories I knew of the Distant Early Warning (DEW) Line, a series of radar installations in far northern Canada that served as sentries for North American airspace.

Fortunately, there was another time that NORAD was in the news: Christmas Eve. For as long as I can remember, radio stations began broadcasting Santa's whereabouts on Christmas Eve just after dinner (local time). The reports were provided by NORAD, which used its radar systems and airplane squadrons to track Santa's progress around the world.

For a young boy, hearing that Santa had just left the UK and was en route to Greenland was proof that he was coming to my house later that night. After all, if the officials at NORAD could actually see him with his sleigh and reindeer in the air, it had to be true.

Many years later I came across NORAD's online Santa tracker. It's a website that graphically depicts Santa's progress around the globe on Christmas Eve. The first time I saw it brought back memories of the live radio reports I used to wait for each year. It made me wonder if youngsters felt the same sense of wonder online as I used to feel standing in the kitchen.

Today you can track Santa using NORAD's website (www.noradsanta.org), which partners with Microsoft, or you can use Google's tracking system (santatracker.google.com). Both websites provide far more than just Santa's location. For example, they provide Christmas-themed games, interactive maps of Santa's village at the North Pole, and a real-time countdown to Santa's arrival.

I found the NORAD/Microsoft website better than the Google website. The former is reminiscent of classic Christmas TV shows like "Rudolph the Red-Nosed Reindeer." The latter feels more like "South Park," right down to the crude graphics. Both websites are very "busy," perhaps catering to today's generation with shorter attention spans.

A definite improvement over earlier versions of the websites is the incorporation of real maps, including Google Street View, to display Santa's location. Even better, you can see what Santa sees from his sleigh as he zooms through the major cities in the world and across far-away landscapes. Like the old NORAD radio reports, seeing actual imagery superimposed on eight reindeer and one man in a red suit makes his journey feel very real.

After all, if Santa can be seen on Google Earth, it has to be true.

LOOKING BACK AT 2014

Hacks, Fracks, and Quacks

Published as "Looking back at 2014's hacks, fracks, setbacks"

December 26, 2014 (433 words)

As the year comes to a close it's time to take a look back at some of the biggest technology stories of 2014. Increased computerization of most aspects of modern life means we're spoiled for choice. However, three items clearly stood out: hacks, fracks, and quacks.

Hacks: In 2014, security vulnerabilities in computer systems affecting multiple sectors were exploited by hackers like never before. Sony's recent travails over its movie "The Interview" are just the most recent example of a yearlong deluge of news items related to cyberattacks. In Sony's case, hackers tried to blackmail them into canceling the release of the movie about the assassination of the leader of North Korea by leaking embarrassing emails from executives, releasing personal information about employees, and by stealing numerous films not yet released and posting them on file sharing websites worldwide.

Earlier in the year Home Depot, Target, Community Health Systems (the parent company of Wuesthoff), and numerous other companies reported losses of customer information such as credit card information due to hacks into their systems. Malware was installed on checkout terminals, websites were defaced, and internal networks were breached seemingly with ease. If these serious flaws don't push organizations to beef up their online security systems, I don't know what will – short of class-action lawsuits or government intervention.

Fracks: If you've filled up your car at the pump recently you'll have been pleasantly surprised at how low the cost of fuel has become. The price of a barrel of oil dropped below $60 recently, a significant drop from just six months ago. It appears the gloomy forecasts of "peak oil" and $10 a gallon gas were way off the mark.

A major contributing factor to the drop in oil prices is the massive increase in domestic production through the use of hydraulic fracturing (fracking). The US leads the way in this innovative approach to energy extraction, which relies on sophisticated technology to access hydrocarbons locked in shale formations deep underground. It's no exaggeration to say that fracking has changed the global socio-political landscape dramatically.

Quacks: Doctors are called upon to serve in capacities that most of us would find difficult. The good Samaritans who volunteer in Doctors Without Borders are an excellent example of this, and perhaps no more so than this year for those who battled the Ebola outbreak in West Africa. This terrible disease is still ravaging that part of the world, and it has shown itself to be annoyingly resistant to modern medicine.

Let's hope for a technological breakthrough in 2015. We've conquered terrible diseases before; we can do it again.

ABOUT THE AUTHOR

Scott Tilley is Professor & Director of Computing Education in the Department of Education and Interdisciplinary Studies at the Florida Institute of Technology. He is an ACM Distinguished Lecturer. His research focuses on software testing, cloud computing, educational technology, and STEM outreach. He writes the weekly "Technology Today" column for the *Florida Today* newspaper (Gannett). His most recent book is *Testing iOS Apps with HadoopUnit: Rapid Distributed GUI Testing* (Morgan & Claypool, 2014).